LANDSCAPE OBSERVATORY
The Work of Terence Harkness

Edited by **M. ELEN DEMING**

APPLIED
RESEARCH
+DESIGN
PUBLISHING

Publisher: AR+D
an imprint of ORO Editions

Novato, CA
www.oroeditions.com
info@oroeditions.com

Publishers of Architecture, Art, and Design

Printed in China

Library of Congress Catalog Card Number
ISBN: 978-1-939621-92-4
10 9 8 7 6 5 4 3 2 1 First Edition

ORO Editions
Gordon Goff: Publisher
info@oroeditions.com
(415) 883.3300

CONTENTS

Landscape Observatory
par excellence

Gary Hilderbrand

We all know the reward that comes with discovery of a designed landscape project that, whether subtly or radically transformative, seems to have risen out of its place—and makes you see the place more acutely, more profoundly. To achieve this, designers must dig into the dynamic characteristics of the territories in which we work, conceptualize their parts, and reorder them with exacting material specificity to make something beautifully fit. Terry Harkness has shown us how to do this and this book is a welcome reflection on his body of thought and work. Whether you have known him as a teacher or colleague, or if you have had only brief encounters, you come to revere the power of his example.

Ten years ago, I spent a long weekend with Terry and a handful of other colleagues reviewing professional awards submissions, debating the worthiness of diverse projects whose authors sought the competitive holy grail of peer recognition. We had little time for banter, but over the course of our days together I learned that Terry had driven his trusty station wagon from Illinois to Washington so he could revisit places and passages he hadn't seen in some years. His itinerary included the familiar agricultural plains of eastern Illinois and central Ohio; the corrugated ridge-and-valley formations along the Allegheny Plateau and Appalachian Mountains of West Virginia, Pennsylvania, and eastern Maryland; and the rolling Piedmont plain that runs to the fall line, where the Potomac meets the coastal plain and bathes Washington's political landscape in thick, humid air. It's fitting that landscape architects convene in the nation's capital annually to judge works from across the US and beyond. For Terry, it matters how you get there.

The trip is 700 miles from Champaign to the coast and takes 11 hours on the road to complete. Perhaps longer if you like to explore. My flight from Boston to Washington had taken just over an hour; I'd commandeered an aisle seat where I could squeeze in some correspondence and review details about our assignment for the weekend deliberations. I wasn't on the plane to observe. But Terry made that trip by car so he could see where he was going—his way of preparing for the jury. Upon learning this, I felt he was rather better equipped than I was to scour the awards submissions for what was really behind them.

Terry was an influential voice for all of us on the jury. He was skeptical of polished photographs and catchy narratives. He argued for deeply felt, conceptualized landscape thinking over well-honed conventions or scratchy innovations. I'd already known Terry's penetrating ways since first seeing his work in the 1986 exhibition, *Transforming the American Garden*. However, all the participants came away from the jury weekend knowing that Terry's interrogative practice had made him an agile design critic, a rigorous cross-examiner and persuasive advocate, a consequential teacher, and, above all, a generous humanist.

What the authors have captured in this book is a heartfelt, wonderfully rich tribute to the real McCoy. There's no hiding the admiration on these pages for Terry's deeply rooted passions, nor the authors' collective appreciation—we might say *envy*—of his teachings. Stories like those told here can emerge only from close knowledge of the man himself from prolonged shared times, and described through well-considered scholarly frameworks and close reading of practice. The authors remind us that Terry's pedagogy in particular gains from the profound influence of Stanley White and the probing ruminations of Bob Riley—two other giants who have enriched and distilled the DNA of the Illinois landscape tradition. How else, and where else, could this happen? It explains so much about Terry Harkness as a teacher.

But the authors push us well beyond that, to the core of his personal practice. Through these essays, we arrive at a palpably complete picture of a rare hybrid creature. He is the beloved academic who really works with land. The mid-western diviner whose reading of a landscape in Mughal India prospers with the same astute foretelling as his critical appraisal of an Illinois farmstead. An artisan who possesses a farmer's straightforward pragmatism but can deliver a gripping sermon on the poetics of the Midwestern horizon or the emblematic role of the hedgerow in a world history of cultivation practices.

The gift of this book is that the pedagogy and designed works of this teacher-maker-philosopher are cast in a bright light through the reflections of those who have had either long association or a brief close encounter with him. Within these chapters, you will come to understand Terry Harkness as one who makes us see, with sharper eyes and greater powers, *par excellence*.

Acknowledgements

M. Elen Deming

This book, long overdue, pays respect to a man who all but defined the Department of Landscape Architecture at the University of Illinois for nearly four decades. Perhaps because Professor *emeritus* Terry Harkness is principally a plainspoken teacher-designer, rather than a scholar, his work has not been widely recognized in the canon of postmodern and contemporary design. Terry's friends, colleagues, and former students offer this book in an attempt to redress that omission.

Terry has long cherished the dream of writing a book himself, yet as is true for most of us, it can prove difficult to gain enough distance on one's own thinking to give it necessary structure. In 2011, the very best of friends, Frank Clements, suggested I might try to muscle Terry into completing the work. Instead, I offered to edit the volume myself. It should have been produced long before now but for my own delinquencies. Happily, in the duration, a number of people offered support and creative cooperation to curate the best of Terry's built works, drawings, photography, essays, and interviews. Together they present a well-rounded portrait. That said, for any errors and omissions in these pages, responsibility is mine.

Early in the process, Molly Briggs (a new PhD student at the time this project began) worked closely with Terry to organize and interpret his key works and thresholds. Their conversations are beautiful and as Terry "teaches" her his method he seems to discover his own work anew. During 2011-12, Molly transcribed over 12 hours of interviews with Terry, scanned key drawings, and coordinated a retrospective exhibition of Terry's work for the CELA Conference (March 2012). Without Molly's fine instincts and dedication this project would never have come to fruition.

Chapters by Brenda Brown, Frank Clements, Doug Johnston, Ken McCown, and Amita Sinha anchor key stages in Terry's career. When the project was languishing, Brenda Brown offered valuable guidance and encouragement. It was also Brenda who recognized the importance of Terry's 1970 thesis as a cornerstone for his design method. Kathleen Harleman, Robert Riley, and Jim Wescoat offer poignant retrospectives on Terry's impact. Liz Vogel (MLA 2017) has been a vital creative partner in the page design and book production and also contributed several photographs. Matt Torgerson, long-term friend and alumnus of the Landscape Architecture Department at the University of Illinois, generously provided insight and images of the Fargo campus taken by Chicago-based photographer James Steinkamp. Ken McCown, a perceptive photographer in his own right, kindly provided many images that illustrate the regional landscapes to which Terry Harkness is most attached. Finally, we are indebted to Terry himself who, in opening up his life and library, offers a treasure trove from his long and still-active career. Terry has engaged in a remarkable process of self-reflection and epiphany requiring equal parts clarity and courage. My hope is that this is just the first of many studies of Terry's work and that it will be worthy of his trust and patience.

Institutional support for this project has come from several sources. At the University of Illinois the College of Fine & Applied Arts Creative Research Fund and the Department of Landscape Architecture's Stanley White Publication Fund helped support project research assistance (Molly Briggs, PhD 2017) and graphic design (Liz Vogel, MLA 2017). A substantial project award from the Brent and Jean Wadsworth Faculty Research Fund and a grant from the Department of Landscape Architecture have supported the book's high quality images and publication. Finally, my deepest appreciation goes to Sharon Harkness, the KAM Council, and all other contributors to the Terence Harkness Legacy Book Project Fund. Without your generosity Terry's work would have remained simply the stuff of legend.

Introduction

Landscape Observatory:
An Introduction

M. Elen Deming and Molly Catherine Briggs

In the ebb and flow of landscape design theory, currents of regionalism remain insistent. Since the late 19th century, in the work of Charles Eliot Jr., Warren Manning, Jens Jensen, Richard Haag, A.E. Bye and Lawrence Halprin, among many others, histories of the American designed landscape are marbled with regionalist values. Similar sensibilities are manifested in the work of master designer Terence G. Harkness (1939–). In his thought process, design work, and teaching, Harkness slips around and beyond his own time, simultaneously of his milieu yet also transcending it.

Harkness's work responds to a moment in landscape architecture when cultural geographers, critics, and historians such as J.B. Jackson, Robert Riley, and William Cronon advanced strong intellectual influences on the field, even as postmodern designers explored the limits of formal and allusive processes. Yet Harkness's practice grows out of very particular intimacies—with a land grant university in East Central Illinois, the epic landscapes of the northern American plains, the fluid pulses of northern California's mountain topographies. While remaining uniquely synthetic, his method offers clear parallels to the work of other place-based designers, for example Warren Byrd or Christophe Girot. In his keen powers of observation, analysis of regional patterns, and best transformation of landscape cues into new representations of place, Harkness's body of work may be characterized as a landscape observatory.

A Pedagogy of Seeing. The notion of the observatory speaks to Harkness's penchant for design as a form of teaching—to compel us to "come to attention" and really see the landscape we inhabit. The objective of such precise perception is not limited to ecological process but, rather, leads to holistic comprehension of landscape genesis, cultural co-evolution, and social formation. Not quite an ecologist, yet far more than a formalist, Harkness's design forms invoke the interdependence of regional cultural history taking place within the biophysical landscape.

Opposite: Prairie Slope Garden at Temple Hoyne Buell Hall, University of Illinois, Champaign-Urbana (photo by L. Brian Stauffer, courtesy of University of Illinois Public Affairs)

Interview with Molly Briggs and M. Elen Deming, August 15, 2011:

MCB: Both disciplinary and yet also transcending that, this idea of observation and observatory seems to be a beautiful way to get beyond the moorings of a single site.

TGH: Right. It is. It's behind all my statements ... or the questions I'm asking myself – can a garden do that? Well, it's really asking: Now can we come to attention? Can we observe and can there be instruments made that assist us

Perhaps typical for his generation (but better than anyone), Harkness explains and teaches through drawing. His drawings express rigorous observation and analysis and inform his earliest teaching activities—whether the history of world landscapes or capstone planting design. His drawings serve as tools—like telescopes or viewing platforms—that simplify, amplify, and offer new perspectives on unintelligibly large patterns. Just as an observatory affords an abstract inventory of key features we're meant to understand, Terry's drawings

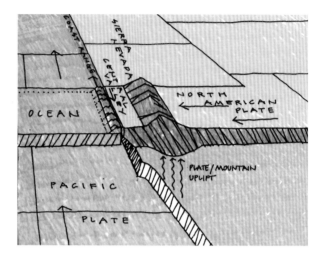

crisply identify what is important—the characteristic logic of form, order, scale, plant associations, soils, water, ambiance. In this way, Harkness makes regional processes and cultural practices, geological tectonic structures, fluvial hydrology, and plant succession seem perfectly legible. As he puts it, "Landscape observatories provide a lens, an experiential window onto our past and present." By showing drainage patterns, shelterbelts, or epic horizon lines, his designs directly engage owners or visitors in site recognition. Indeed, the clarity of his analysis and subsequent synthesis of form is a kind of landscape pedagogy in itself, allowing others to form eidetic connections well beyond the site, toward a critical awareness of region.

Interview with Molly Briggs and M. Elen Deming, August 15, 2011:

TGH: *[Molly] asked me the question, why did you use the term observatory? I had gotten so far away from it. I was talking about the same project as both a park and a garden, but there was an evolution of that project where the whole idea of what an observatory is, is what we're trying to make. It's the lens by which you see experience and land and observatories are built exactly to do that. So they are these renaissance machines, or devices through which you begin to see in a new way. ... So she forced me to say that much more self-consciously. And that was very useful actually, to ask that question.*

MED: *So it seems [Observatory] is a metaphor for what this book is, as well as what your practice is, as well as the tools you make within your practice.*

Having been mentored and molded by his predecessors at the University of Illinois at Urbana-Champaign—the legendary Stanley White and Robert Riley among them—Harkness began a remarkable 40+ year teaching career fresh out of graduate school. The magnetism and charisma evinced by truly great teachers often manifest the depths of their character. In his later nomination for ASLA's 2007 Jot Carpenter Teaching Medal, colleagues and students describe Harkness as a man of "quiet integrity" and "a beacon of enthusiasm" with "lively intellectual curiosity." Certainly, for many, Harkness is a living legend, prairie savant, and heir to the legacy of great teaching at the University of Illinois.

The long arc of Harkness's design practice and teaching is important because it is devoted to a practice perhaps best termed by the architect Kenneth Frampton as *critical regionalism*. Frampton argues for analytical, poetic, and material resistance to generic, mechanistic, and universalizing expression in design, which he refers to as "the victory of universal civilization over locally inflected culture."[1] Conversely, landscape architecture operates as something other than regionalist when it is globalist and generalized or, in Harkness's words, "casual, fragmented, a-spatial, and generic."[2]

Offering a compelling rationale in support of cultural sustainability and landscape performance agendas, critical regionalism remains relevant today. In the late 1970s and early '80s, Frampton recognized that landscape heritage and regionally inspired design might challenge the placelessness of architectural practices that dominated design in mid-century America. Yet regionalism continues to offer alternatives to what are now termed drosscapes and logistical landscapes. The systems and structures of mass globalization accelerate the wholesale destruction of heritage communities and vernacular landscape patterns. This is not to suggest that regionalism is anti-modern. Rather, in its contemporary range and diversity of formal design treatments, it should be understood as a grounded form of modernism—a process neither utopian nor universal, but instead pragmatic and particular. In Harkness's practices, we might simply think of regionalism as design with staying power.

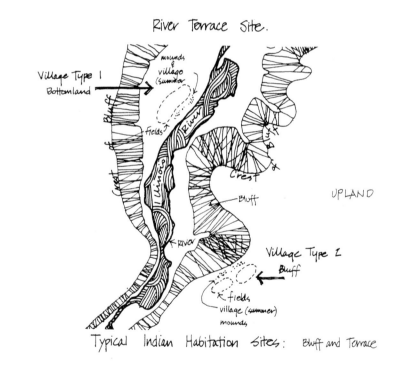

Typical Indian Habitation Sites: Bluff and Terrace

Harkness's emerging regionalist design approach was already clearly telegraphed by his Masters thesis: *A Landscape in Evolution: The Graphic History of Champaign and Piatt Counties From 70,000 B.C. to A.D. 1860*. It is still considered one of the best and most comprehensive guides to the Midwestern landscape ever written (see Brown 30-33). The ambition of the thesis is startling, revealing the scope and sensibility of a geographer-artist and the clarity of a master teacher. However, it is important to recognize that the very best of his mature projects build—technically, formally, intellectually—on the foundation of this thesis.

Harkness readily admits it took a long time for him to crystallize his signature approach. Having cut his teeth as an entry-level instructor at the University of Illinois (1969-73), Harkness left teaching for several years to explore professional design practice at HOK (St. Louis, Missouri). While at HOK, Harkness created designed environments within a regional geomorphic, biotic, and cultural context. He also streamlined his analysis process along with a characteristic place-based vocabulary of form, pattern, and scale for design proposals (see Clements and Deming 18-29). In 1981, then in his early forties, he returned to the University of Illinois where he began to pursue a series of deep explorations into cultural context, natural process, and designed landscapes—essentially, as he puts it, "to figure out what I was trying to do." Where Part I of this book provides an orientation to Terry's overall values and trajectory, his remarkable mid- to late-career explorations comprise the content of Part II, the Portfolio section of this book.

The Portfolio and Essays.

Illinois Gardens. Drawn from a series of Harkness's midwestern explorations he called Gardens From Region, the Illinois gardens combine an iterative analysis of vernacular forms with other scale experiments in material construction such as the Workingman's Garden (see Johnston 36-45). The project culminated in a set of drawings selected for exhibition at the Harvard Graduate School of Design and for subsequent publication in *Transforming the American Garden*, the catalog curated and edited by Michael Van Valkenburgh (1986-1988). His experiences in Japan prepared Harkness to define the "borrowed landscape," that is the surrounding agricultural patterns, as an integral part of the Illinois garden. The inner gardens draw their character from that larger space—their ambience, seasonality, and larger spatial ecologies flow from the borrowed landscape beyond.

There may be some commensurate risk in distilling the everyday, especially if success in design is measured by a kind of invisibility. This caveat is suggested by Treib, who writes: "Terence Harkness's 'An East Central Illinois Garden' is refreshing in its humility and all but loses its identity in the cultivated fields that surround it."[3] Rather than becoming lost in its surrounding landscape, we would argue, *An East Central Illinois Garden* only intensifies it. It is of the surrounding landscape, as the Miller Garden is of the landscape of Columbus, Indiana. Like looking into the wrong end of a telescope, this garden draws everything to itself in miniature, while also making us see those close things as somehow distant—and part of a vastly larger system.

Below right: Terry Harkness, n.d. Detail from "Garden Zones" of the East Central Illinois Garden project

Opposite from top:

Terry Harkness, n.d. Detail from "Topographic Domains," Foothill Mountain Observatory; Terry Harkness, n.d. Alluvial Fan/ Outwash Arroyo/Park Entry—detail from Foothill Mountain Observatory; Yamuna River benchmarks, erosion control, and flood detritus next to 16th century Mughal garden pavilion; conservation zone north of the Taj Mahal (photo courtesy of Ken McCown, 2002)

Foothill Mountain Observatory*.* A decade later, Harkness's synthetic regionalist approach was cast in glorious relief by his co-curation (with Brenda Brown and Doug Johnston) of *Eco-revelatory Design: Nature Constructed / Nature Revealed*, a traveling exhibition that debuted at the University of Illinois and was later published as a special issue of *Landscape Journal* (1996-98). This landmark symposium, catalog, and national exhibition concluded its three-year run by landing at the National Building Museum in Washington, D.C. The project represents an effort to define ecological design as "that which considers issues attendant to the interactive processes and dynamic balance among organisms and their environment" and "reveals and interprets ecological phenomena, processes and relationships."[4]

Among the highlights of the Eco-Revelatory exhibition was *Foothill Mountain Observatory: Reconsidering Golden Mountain*—a dream landscape inspired by Harkness's boyhood landscape (see McCown 46-55). The project itself was the culmination of a sabbatical leave Harkness took in the mid-1990s, in part to recover and revitalize his design research after suffering a lengthy illness. *Observatory* proposes a park at the foot of the San Gabriel Mountains, a range Robert Thayer describes as the "fastest uplifting and fastest eroding mountain range in North America."[5] The park is designed to allow visitors to compare managed and unmanaged regimes including the "ecosystemics of mountain building and erosion, fault lines, earthquakes, mass movement, alluvial fans, debris flows, storms, flash flooding and flood control, fire ecology, prescribed burning, plant communities, agriculture, and human culture."[6] In *Observatory*, tectonic, biotic, and fluvial forces are all rendered visible, expressed vividly through a garden series with a variety of managed and unconstrained dimensions.

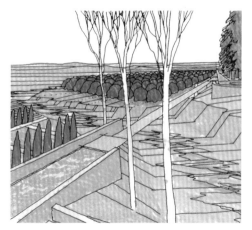

Taj Mahal Cultural Heritage District. Harkness's productivity has never been limited to speculative work; in fact, he has demonstrated spectacularly patient long-term and large-scale vision for several projects still being realized. Among them, his planning and design leadership for the Taj Mahal World Heritage site in India must certainly be acknowledged. At Taj Mahal, Harkness worked on the development of the Cultural Heritage District Master Plan with a team of Illinois faculty, students, and local contacts, with repeat visits over several years from the late 1990s to the early 2000s (see Sinha 56-63). His formative explorations as a student in Japan helped Harkness understand the Taj Mahal as a contested cultural monument within a dynamic riparian ecology. Harkness systematically studied visual and ambient experiences for several hundred acres of the Yamuna River flood plain, walking it repeatedly, students in tow, in order to understand local values, vantage points, visitors' expectations, competing economic uses, and cultural meanings in the context of sometimes extreme climatic pulses. And in observing how the Taj performs as a "figure"—a kind of architecture body in space—he showed the team how it orients landscape, vision, and cultural desire toward its looming, sometimes ghostly presence.

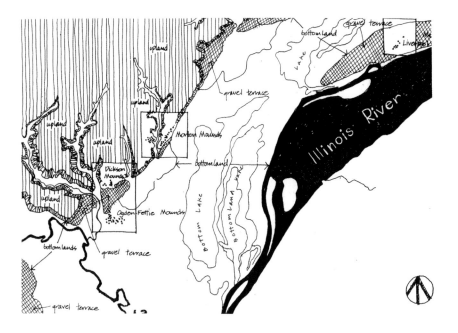

Emiquon. The Emiquon Nature Preserve is a 7,000-acre regional natural area near Havana, Illinois, managed by the Nature Conservancy along the Illinois River. In consultation with faculty colleague Doug Johnston and landscape architecture alumnus Austin Tao (Tao & Associates, St. Louis), Harkness developed an interpretive plan for visitors to Emiquon (see Johnston 64-71). Hydrological, natural, and cultural histories are addressed in the proposal, including data visualization showing changes in surface and subsurface water patterns at the site. In many ways an extension of what was learned at the Taj Mahal, Harkness and partners considered how visitors move through the site and apprehend not only the ecological processes, but also the cultural history of the floodplain's use over time. In this way, the project design permits different locations throughout the preserve to function explicitly as landscape observatories: the Heritage Observatory, the Woodland Observatory, the Wetland Observatory, and the Water Management Observatory. In this series of designed encounters, this huge preservation area is both cajoled and disciplined into revealing its distinct cultural and natural histories to visitors.

Above: Harkness, Johnston, and Tao, 2006. Emiquon landscape analysis, Emiquon Nature Preserve (Odgen Fettie, Dickson, Morton, and Liverpool Mounds, p. 35, Visitor Use Plan Technical Report)

Right: Terry Harkness. Landscape design for International Software, Fargo, ND (photo courtesy of Brenda Brown, 2015)

International Software. At International Software, a fast-growing regional corporate campus in the northern plains, Harkness translates yet another regional landscape type into an observatory for comprehending natural process, climatic and seasonal change, remnants of cultural practices (shelterbelts, drainage lines, farm buildings, and field succession) and the subtle glories of regional ephemera (see Brown 72-81). Beginning as the corporate headquarters of Great Plains Software, the campus has been further developed for International Software in Fargo, North Dakota. In collaboration with site manager Matt Torgerson, Harkness designed and detailed the landscape treatments for signature buildings by architects Julie Snow (Julie Snow Architects) and Ralph Johnson (Perkins & Will). Harkness explains, "our ability as designers to tell stories of the landscape and the culture in an abstracted, distilled way" was the main challenge of this project. His love affair with this place is evident in his own narrative:

Eastern North Dakota is a landscape of sky, light, expanse and variability. The sunset fire on the sky and flat horizon establish the power of the northern plains. Modulating the clear, crisp northern air and light is the vertical definition of repeating bands of densely planted shelterbelts, a response to the devastating drought and dust-bowl conditions of the 1930s. In summer foliage, the shelterbelts define spacious, comfortable rooms; in the winter, the dormant trees define a screen silhouetted against the sky or snow-covered fields, as Robert Irwin's temporary scrim installations revealed presence and light. Marking the ground plane of this flat lakebed landscape is a network of shallow drainways and deep ditch lines. ...The quicksilver pattern of water threads and strands appears at spring melt or following summer's more intense thunderstorms. Punctuating this horizontal scene are precisely constructed cubes, rectangles and cylinders of homes, machine sheds, storage bins and farm buildings.[7]

A Grounded Phenomenology.

Perhaps because the clarity and rigor of his approach exists principally in his drawings and pedagogy, rather than in published texts or a large body of built work—or perhaps, too, because he resides in the 'fly-over' region of the great continental United States—Harkness's legacy has been largely overlooked. Yet as Joan Nassauer puts it, his career "is a star shining from deep space: he has cared much more about both the exploration of ideas and integrity of actions than about his personal recognition." This book is an overdue attempt to spotlight his design research and working methods for a new generation of designers to whom his work may be instructive and encouraging.

Landscape architecture seems caught between the paradigms of globalism, scientism, data visualization, and technological virtuosity on the one hand and, on the other, demands for grounded landscape performance and the scaled exigencies of development. But great designers forever change the way society observes and thus inhabits the landscape. Avoiding the false dichotomies of nature and culture, Harkness taught two generations of students how to observe the interdependency between landscape form and cultural process, to mediate contingency while maintaining the role of landscape as a medium of sensitive formal interpretations of place, phenomena, and region.

Reconsidering the career of Terence Harkness in terms of critical regionalism affords a golden opportunity to reflect on the current state of professional education and the enduring necessity for teaching design. In the following pages, we present selections from Harkness's built works, unbuilt drawings, published essays, lecture notes, diagrams, photography, and in-depth interviews as a basis for understanding and evaluating Harkness's impact and trajectory in design, research, and pedagogy. We hope this work may contribute to contemporary debates weighing the commitment of landscape architecture to place-based design and/or to more abstract systems-based approaches.

[1] *Kenneth Frampton, 1983. "Towards a critical regionalism: Six points for an architecture of resistance," in The Anti-Aesthetic: Essays on Postmodern Culture. Seattle: Bay Press. 17.*
[2] *Terry Harkness, 1990. "Garden From Region," in The Meaning of Gardens. ed. M. Francis and R. Hester. Cambridge: MIT Press, 110.*
[3] *Marc Treib, 1986. "On Paper and Plants [An Exhibition Debate]," Places: Transforming the American Garden vol 3:3, 57.*
[4] *Brown, Harkness, Johnston. 1998. Original 1994 exhibition "Proposal." Reprinted in Eco-Revelatory Design: Nature Constructed/Nature Revealed. Special Issue of Landscape Journal, x.*
[5] *Robert L. Thayer, Jr. 1998. "Landscape as an Ecologically Revealing Language." In Eco-Revelatory Design: Nature Constructed/Nature Revealed. Special Issue of Landscape Journal. 126.*
[6] *Thayer. ibid. 127.*
[7] *Terry Harkness, 2004. "Distilling North Dakota," Landscape Architecture Magazine vol 84:4 (April), 66.*

Formative Landscapes:
Biographical Notes on Terry Harkness

By Frank C. Clements with M. Elen Deming

As a landscape architect, Terence (Terry) Harkness is a unique synthesis of "California modernist" with "Midwestern sensibilities." His work demonstrates his respect and concern for the health of the land, its people and cultures, and his recognition of the inherent beauty of their relationships and interdependencies. Harkness's personal history begins in his Southern California childhood. He was fascinated by exploring, on foot and bicycle, the gridiron pattern of Pasadena as it meets and negotiates the slopes and canyons of the foothills of the San Gabriel Mountains. The imprint of Pasadena may help explain the sensitivity demonstrated in his midwestern work; arguably, because he was not originally from the prairie region, he was able to see its contrasting character so very clearly.

After studying landscape architecture at the University of Illinois in the late 1960s, Harkness embraced regionalist values in his design speculations, built works, and teaching, all of which incorporate an exquisite awareness of place-based processes. The year before completing his MLA degree, while on a Ryerson Fellowship study tour, Harkness studied the canon of Japanese temples and gardens, an experience that shaped the way he thought of landscape form, vision, and experience for the remainder of his long career. However, the development of his feeling for landscape is expressed beautifully by Terry himself, in his contribution to a *Landscape Journal* compilation called "Most Influential Landscapes" (1993). Editors Robert Riley and Brenda Brown asked a group of leading designers "what landscapes ... not more than three ... have been most influential/important to you in your work, and why/how?" Below is Terry's response:

Above: Terence G. Harkness (1939–) (photo courtesy of Terence Harkness)

Opposite: Outwash fan from mountain stream (photo courtesy of Ken McCown, April 2017)

With great affection and intimacy, three American landscapes have been important and influential to my experiences as an avid landscape observer. One is of the days growing up in the foothill communities of Southern California at the base of the San Gabriel mountain range. The annual summer vacations spent at my parents' family homes along the bluffs of the Mississippi River were another. These early experiences shaped and sharpened my enthusiasm for three realms of my life. One is the fascination and wonder of the natural structure of landscape—climate, geomorphology, plants. The second is the human interaction and adaptation of agrarian enterprise and the natural context. The third is the built patterns of our homes, streets and neighborhoods that make our cities. The contrast and evolution of landscapes is always a revealing statement of our presence, persistence, and aspirations.

Southern California was the discovery on foot and bicycle of several worlds. The mountain slopes, ridges, and cool canyons of the San Gabriel were a wonder. Happening upon abandoned trails overgrown by chaparral or mountain cabins in upper ravines was the discovery of lost history. Nightfall panoramas overlooking the valley basins below was [sic] the paradox of physical separation and simultaneous visual inclusion. The sense of risk, a catastrophic landscape of earthquake, rockslides and bush fire was always in dramatic contrast to the daily experience of benign, endless sunny days and shadowing live oak trees. The well-shaded streets of Pasadena marked a gridiron pattern ascending the slopes to the base of the mountains. Exploring arroyos and open washes within the city by bicycle one would later discover that those homes had been the work of the Green brothers, Irving Gill, or a house by Frank Lloyd Wright. Or going to the Pasadena library was visiting the later civic and residential architecture of Myron Hunt. Set around or beside these two aspects of landscape were the orange or avocado orchards, vineyards, or dairies located on the alluvial fans far below the mountain range.

My parents were the nomadic American family moving up, moving on, and moving out—restlessly seeking some better place or job. The Southern California landscape of earthquakes and sun were in stark opposition to the memorable verdant greens of summers spent on the farms of my aunts and uncles in the rural Middle West. The agricultural adventure of fields, real woods, swimming in cool permanent streams and ponds, was a landscape education in a dramatically different climate region and vegetational exuberance. Each place had a powerful openness, distinctive geologic and topographic structure. This education of travel has nurtured a curiosity and sympathy for places that is unending.

But this abiding context of place, travel, and discovery cannot overshadow a third memorable landscape of my life and imagination—the intensive years of sandbox. This was my childhood fixation. From crawling onward, the sandbox was my apprenticeship, journeymanship, and high level practice in landscape creation. This mildly obsessive work was about experiment and continual revision. I distinctly recall the seriousness of this work when I was able to convince my best friend's father to drive us fifty miles in search of that elusive material—the perfect sand-soil combination for shaping and molding streets, mountains, tunnels, and towns. This essential ingredient for our sandbox made it the envy of the neighborhood.

Perhaps we relive our feeling and experience of the landscapes of our youth. We often project these feelings forward to what we now imagine or desire to create. This past background is the raw material and measure of what we wish to reveal in our new places. In these futures we hope and are often compelled to create places that speak to those of the past. An underlying interest in knowing places and the desire to create fresh ones is so that others might recognize and enjoy them as shared feeling and accomplishment (1993, 176-77).

Above: *Live oak groves. (photo courtesy of Terence G. Harkness, ca. 1995)*

Opposite: *Transitional landscapes in the foothill communities of the San Gabriel range; clockwise, Orange grove with irrigation channel, Desert botanical collection at Huntington Gardens, Pasadena, Agrarian allée of Eucalyptus trees (photo courtesy of Terence G. Harkness, ca. 1995)*

Intellectual Influences. Terry's designs are driven more by project context than by any rigid design philosophy. Given the environmental, aesthetic, and cultural context of the site, the clients' desires, program, and budget, he always asks the same questions: "What is the site telling us?" and therefore "What does the design want to be?" After a thorough analysis and synthesis of site conditions in context, Terry produces multiple schemes that may be evaluated, ranked, and discussed for their salient points. Terry explains his approach as the result of living not in a black and white world, but in a gray world with few absolutes. There may be "A-ha!" moments in Terry's design process, but no lighting bolts of pre-determination. There is definitely an ego, perhaps even some preconceived ideas, but they are always relegated to the background.

Asking the right questions can, or must, be a strong enough rationale to guide the discovery of design responses. Terry always has to understand why something is what it is. He is constantly studying and researching everything under the sun. Some of this was born out of the research environment he found at the University of Illinois as well as contemporary trends in landscape architecture emerging in the early 1980s and '90s. Landscape architects were always questioning the effects of their designs, how their impacts could be measured and improved. Their investigations ranged from questions of aesthetic beauty to in-depth scientific understanding of environments and understanding human perceptual needs as determinants for design. Today we might call this evidence-based design. For Terry, it's nothing new.

Interview with Molly Briggs and M. Elen Deming, August 1 and 8, 2011:

TGH: The foundational book for me was May Watts's Reading the Landscape. And Jackson's magazine Landscape was the same kind of thing. And books … about plants, knowing plants.

But still [the field of landscape architecture] had no theory base. Bob Riley wrote about this and people decried it and a bunch of wonderful people said, if we don't have a theoretical base for what we're doing, then we're not going to get any better at what we do. So this was all going on. I had nothing to contribute to that. But this is before … 1980. And then things [started happening] … people who were doing things with theory bases behind them, like Michael Van Valkenburgh's garden exhibit at Harvard and Beth Meyer [now at UVA]. Let's look at The Meaning of Gardens, by Mark Francis and Randy Hester. And then there were some historians; Marc Treib is absolutely brilliant, cranky as hell but brilliant.

So this is what's going on. All this dissatisfaction. That's what Bob did, he's so thoughtful. … Cultural geography. Cosgrove, Daniels, J.B. Jackson! That was just a huge thing for me and for Bob and for a bunch of people. … Catherine Howett in the Eco-Revelatory catalog caught the breadth of LA history and theory, talks about everybody. And Brenda [Brown]'s piece in there is an exhaustive overview. Those two pieces really set the panorama of theory in the field since 1950 ….

How did Eco-Revelatory work get started? Doug [Johnston] and Jory Johnson wrote a seminal piece … why there were no examples of work that showed the integration of ecology and design. And that's when we started Eco-Revelatory. We didn't think you did ecology and design separately; they ought to talk to each other. But there were no examples you could show students. A few artists had done some work, there is a part of the catalog that talks about the artists who did that, and you know all of them. So Eco-Rev was a reaction to no critical theory and ... to no discussion of landscape architectural design and ecology ... and because there ought to be something thoughtful about it done. We were sitting down and said where will we take students to see stuff? You can do make believe stuff all you want but you finally have to take them somewhere. ... So this is the climate that I grew into.

During our many discussions in graduate school and in working together for over 45 years, more times than I can count, Terry has mentioned several landscape architects and individuals in other disciplines who have influenced his thinking. First, Terry credits Phil Lewis who, with his regional recreational and cultural resource plans for Illinois and Wisconsin, helped develop Terry's initial interest in landscape architecture. For upon first seeing Phil's work, Terry saw all the things he liked to do and was interested in: drawing, building, plants, and the study of landscapes in their natural environment. His initial idea of taking a major in history quickly became a thing of the past. He wanted to be better informed and educated about the natural world, how it was formed and designed, and the aesthetics of place.

Terry often credited Florence Bell Robinson as a major influence on his approach and appreciation of plants and plantings in the Midwest. Robinson was the first woman faculty member at UIUC Department of Landscape Architecture (indeed she was the first tenured woman professor at any accredited school of landscape architecture) and author of several works on planting design such as *Useful Trees and Shrubs* (1st ed. 1938), the classic card file on hardy woody plants. Terry also cited Brian Hackett, a faculty member whose ecological approach to planting design influenced him profoundly. Other influential professors at UIUC included Stan White, Hideo Sasaki, Don Walker, Natalie Alpert, and, later in his career, Doug Johnston.

A year before he completed his MLA degree, Terry was transformed by his 1969 Ryerson Fellowship in Japan. Robert Riley, then incoming Head of the Department of Landscape Architecture recounts that Terry "got the Ryerson Traveling Fellowship rules changed. He was the first [student] allowed to go to Japan, not Europe." In his own synthetic way, Terry knew that the traditional Grand Tour of European monuments was not what he was seeking, not what he needed just then. But his travels were transformative and, through them, Terry experienced what he calls "essential notions of landscape and place."

Terry's relationship with Bob Riley also deeply imprinted his work for years to come. When Bob Riley first came to Illinois, fresh off the road from Santa Fe as associate editor at J.B. Jackson's *Landscape* magazine, he transformed what was going on in the department. As a cultural geographer, Jackson had inspired Terry to understand geomorphology as well as cultural patterns in the landscape. In fact, Jackson's famous rides through the landscape on his motorcycle may have inspired Terry to take his own, equally famous cross-country road trips throughout the West and Midwest. As Terry likes to remind us, he traveled back and forth to the west coast over fifty times. His vanity plates "open roads" tell us about his love for trips.

Below: Robert B. Riley (1931-) (photo courtesy of the University of Illinois Archives)

Multi-Disciplinary Design—the HOK Years.

There are so many dimensions to Terry's work—not just the speculative gardens for which he is justly admired. Terry worked more than seven years (1974—1981) at HOK Architects (formerly Hellmuth, Obata, and Kassabaum), a large firm with a global practice base, where he was named Senior Vice President in charge of Design and Planning. His St. Louis practice garnered national design and planning recognition for Terry and his colleagues, especially from the American Planning Association for his work on the 1980 Winter Olympics facilities at Lake Placid, New York, and the American Society of Landscape Architects for Lacledes Landing, the popular St. Louis riverfront redevelopment.

In *Architecture in the Real World: The Work of HOK* (1984), Walter McQuade vividly describes the multi-disciplinary design world of the St. Louis-based firm. HOK is a design-driven practice with real world business challenges: clients with budgets, schedules, and deadlines. More often than not, Terry's work at HOK was subsumed in a larger body of multi-disciplinary design projects such as corporate headquarters, universities, industrial plants, and business parks. Working on multiple project types meant spending time understanding the complexities of each and how to work on fast-track construction projects where time was literally money.

Above from top: Frank Clements (left) and Terry Harkness (right) work on a drawing with a colleague at HOK, late 1970s. St. Louis, MO (photo by Frank Clements). Terry Harkness at his desk at HOK in late 1970s (photo courtesy of Terence G. Harkness)

Right: Frank Clements (left) and Terry Harkness (right) on site, August 1983. Stonegate Development, Fort Worth, Texas (photo courtesy of Frank Clements)

At HOK in the 1970s, the landscape architect was always the first one on site. Gyo Obata (1923-), co-founder and design partner at HOK, dictated that landscape architects should set the framework for all master plans identifying the critical geologic, hydrologic, vegetation, slopes, views, and other cultural issues unique to the site, no matter the size of the site. These parameters drove Terry to develop and formalize a design process he and other landscape architects at HOK came to embrace on all projects at that time. Born out of the necessity of limited budgets and schedules it was used to quickly and efficiently define and inform all site designs. It was an ingenious analysis process that Terry called "Development

Opportunities and Constraints / Environmental Framework Plan." Establishing a landscape 'kit of parts' or tools allowed him to quickly synthesize the natural with the artificial or human-made, and thus combine apparently unrelated objects and images into a larger and more inclusive whole.

The Aetna Life and Casualty Group's U.S. headquarters in Middletown, Connecticut, described in *Architecture in the Real World*, epitomizes the design process Terry developed. He conducted a thorough analysis of the 287-acre site, complete with natural, cultural, and human-made features, zoning limitations, and zones of visual contrasts and opportunities. The resulting 30-page document described the development suitability of the site clearly defining where the buildings and parking lots should go, where natural features should be left as a rural park or environmental preserve. This process resulted in a design appropriate to its site and to its context.

Terry's signature graphics and passion for free-hand drawings were also key to his design process. He understood the importance of graphics in creating a conversation, where landscape could hold its own in the dialogue among designers, clients, and stakeholders. Terry's short form design process and kit-of-parts approach was essential to inform design parameters for each project quickly and efficiently without short-circuiting overall design quality. The formula for a successful project, he felt, was when clients fully understood the design process and the resulting project. Terry's drawings were therefore crucial for achieving client and collaborator buy-in towards a design consensus.

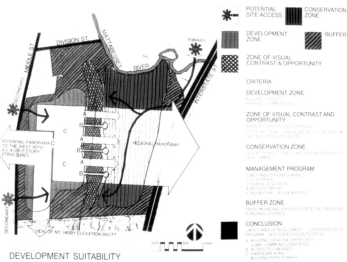

DEVELOPMENT SUITABILITY

Above: Site analysis drawings for the Aetna Group Division Headquarters, Middletown, CN, HOK Architects (photo courtesy of Frank Clements)

Interview with Molly Briggs and M. Elen Deming, August 1, 2011:

MCB: Let's talk about scale. ... You've worked at a variety of scales, and I wonder if you have a favorite scale.

TGH: One garden I was going to build was going to be 300' by 300'. But [at HOK] I worked on the site selection for the Alaskan capital, they were going to move from Juneau; and I worked with a fellow from San Francisco on the site selection process ... for a project that was 40 thousand acres. I will work at any scale and I work really, really hard to be able to work at any scale. The hardest thing that you have to be able to do, whatever scale you work at, is the piece you're doing has got to be right. Whether it's just the entry to a house or a high school, there's a quality of spaciousness and comfort that's right. So I have no preference for scale. But I am paranoid about being correct ... I've spent my lifetime, whenever you do something that you build, you lay it out. You literally lay it out 3 times, 4 times, with stakes or whatever, to get it right.

MCB: And then moving around in it, to see how it works.

TGH: You've got to do that. I can do it now and I hardly ever miss. In the last 10 or 15 years I have been right on the money. But, you just have to do that. It's the same thing when you site something. Is it too far in the ground, too far out of the ground? Thomas Church in Gardens Are For People talks about this as well as anything I've ever read. He talks about the spaciousness of the steps or the width of the entry. How wide a walk should be or how spacious and welcoming each of these things should be. ... he really understood the residential scale. He did the GM Tech Center with Eero Saarinen ... he did the site work for that, Thomas Church, and his gardens are just exquisite. Some of the materials have not aged well, and some of his forms look a little strange, but he understood the spacious, welcoming, generous well-planned design. If it isn't planned well, it doesn't work well ... but when you take that extra care, things have comfort.

Terry's projects at HOK were diverse in scale and program. They ranged from his regional work on the scenic and visual attributes for the State of Alaska Capitol Site Selection project to a land plan for Atajo—a 30,000-acre parcel in southern California. In the years we overlapped, Terry and I collaborated on several corporate campus master plans for big Fortune 500 companies. His analysis technique was instrumental in defining the development framework for Mobil Oil's U.S Division Headquarters in Fairfax Virginia; the Pillsbury Headquarters Site Evaluation Study in Minnesota; and of course, Aetna, among others. The State of Alaska Capital Site Selection Project involved site analysis and selection of three alternate sites all consisting of several thousands of acres of virgin landscapes—quite an amazing once-in-a-lifetime project.

Terry played a key role in the urban design plan for the historic Lacledes Landing on the riverfront, next to the Arch in downtown Saint Louis, and prepared visual improvement plans for several 1000-plus-acre chemical plants throughout the U.S. Regardless of type, however, each project followed his signature design methodology. His portfolio of work at HOK was both prolific and outstanding in its breadth of projects, design innovation and creativity—a body of work most landscape architects would be proud to have created in their lifetime.

Terry's Place in Design History. After nearly a decade in professional practice, Terry Harkness made the decision to return to teaching at the University of Illinois. It was never a repudiation of practice; after all, he never stopped practicing. Rather it was a different kind of investment in himself. As he puts it: "There are two Terry Harknesses. This is the practitioner; this is the speculator. That's why I left practice. I've put them together."

Interview with Molly Briggs and M. Elen Deming, August 1, 2011:

TGH: There was something more I wanted to do. I couldn't get enough [design work] that I was happy with and I couldn't convince anybody! And I can be pretty strong and articulate with designers, because I've always been around architects and I've competed successfully. ... But I thought, these guys are never going to take the work that I think could go to the next level. And I probably stayed a little too long, actually.

When I came back [to the University of Illinois] Bob asked me, "What do you want to do?" I couldn't answer him. I knew exactly the feeling that I wanted the work to be about [but] couldn't put it in words—couldn't define why I came back to teaching, my research agenda. So I said, I don't know what I want to do, but I know what I feel I should be doing. And don't ask me to describe what I feel like I should be doing. That's what I want to do. And he knew me well enough to know what that meant.

That's why it appeals to me when you talk about—what were the words you used—creative research, investigation —that's what it's always been to me, and that's what every project should be. Every project we do, I don't care what it is, what scale. ... Through persistence and stubbornness—I was going to do this! I was going to quit practice, I was going to come back to do this. ... This kind of investigation.

From the perspective of someone who loves the inherent beauty of the Midwestern landscape and makes designs that embrace and enhance and respect its best features with native species, Terry might be compared to Jens Jensen or perhaps O.C. Simonds for his use of plant materials to define and create outdoor rooms. Certainly regionalists Warren Byrd and A.E. Bye have pursued parallel paths in creating a sense of place for natural-looking landscapes and using documentation such as drawing and photography to capture its living essence.

Among living contemporaries, Terry deeply admires Michael Van Valkenburgh (MLA 1978, UIUC) as well as the work of the firm Reed Hilderbrand for their sensitivity to site and appropriately restrained design. Indeed, reading "The Inventions of Reed Hilderband," in the August 2012 issue of LAM, it struck me that Doug Reed and Gary Hilderbrand have embraced many of the same attitudes as Terry. Similarly, they too appear to have some difficulty describing their philosophy of design. I love their story about asking artists to explain their work and they only say, " It's just some red paint." Terry would probably say, "it's just some trees." But Hilderbrand's words echo so many of my conversations with Terry. "Every project is different, but all of our projects are attempts to help people see and know where they are. We investigate the site thoroughly before designing in order to discover what we think should be drawn out and emphasized. We ask: "What is this place? How was it formed? How is it being formed now?" (2012, 82).

Interview with Molly Briggs and M. Elen Deming, August 1, 2011:

MCB: You've said that much of your work draws on the common, everyday landscape of the Midwest, and that design elements are "derived from the common or enduring characteristics of particular scenes in the Midwestern landscape." Do you think that landscape has changed in the time that you've been dealing with it?

TGH: Yes. Oh my gosh, yes! You really notice this when you go to [International Software] up in North Dakota, where they had all the shelterbelts from the '30s, because of the dust storms. You fly and you see it all—the landscape is this wonderful set of rooms. When you fly over it you see these shelterbelts and these houses and you're kind of embedded there. When you're down on the ground, you go from room to room. These are incredible walls of trees. You pass from one to the other and then you finally get to a certain point and you break out of that and it changes, so that there's a scale change or you go up and down and it changes. Here, the farms, right after WWII, were about 200 acres, maybe a little bit more than that. And if you go down to Amish country, right now, you could only farm 200 acres with horses, with animals. That's the size you can do, that's all you can do. So you get fields of that size; you get pastures, whatever the module is has changed. The mile grid is what it was; but the windrows or the hedgerows were a different scale. But all that has come away.

Probably the houses, objects—you know, they were little, trees and clumps—that's changed. The distance between the little towns in no different, it's still about seven to nine miles; but they're dying in many cases, unless they become a little suburb [of a regional economic center] ... [B]ut what's really changed is that the machines are so huge! All of a sudden they're putting down grain in rows or in patterns that are so vivid and powerful when you drive through

AGRARIAN LANDSCAPE

BUILDING VOCABULARY

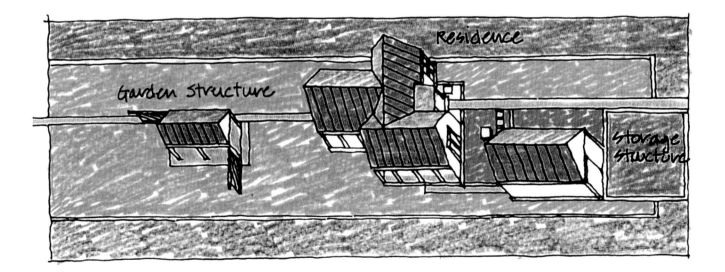

Garden Structure

Residence

Storage Structure

them; in October, when they bring it down, it all opens up. By July it's all closed down. Every year October, about the first or second week in October, I'm out driving around in the country and it's opening up. It just literally opens up, and you lose these hallways and allées. So that has changed, because there used to be all these tree rows, with pheasants. Now it's these big broad spacious flat places with these extraordinary machines and they do [the harvest] in a week. It's a whole scale thing.

In his approach to detailed site-specific design, Terry's love and use of plants is practically unique in design practice today. Plants are not an afterthought in Terry's designs; throughout his career he consistently gives plants a major role to play for establishing the framework or the bones of his designs and avoids the over-use of hardscape elements. While most designers go for the hard and the fast result, Terry draws on the experience and perspective of past greats (such as Olmsted, Jensen, and Simonds) knowing that landscapes take time to evolve into their true mature design character. A confident designer like Terry is in it for the long game: he has the canny patience to wait for his work to take root, mature, and, ultimately, to let his design speak for itself.

For a variety of reasons, compared to his contemporaries in the field, Terry's work is not well known. It simply isn't in his DNA to crave recognition; instead he is more than happy to let others occupy the limelight. But among clients and collaborators, Terry has secured respect and made many friends. His clients are often taken into Terry's own earnest search for the most appropriate design for them. He lets them inside his thought process and includes them in the design process. In doing so, he makes them feel privileged to be treated as equal members of his team and important parts of his inspiration. After all, from nearly four decades as a professor working with students to inform and teach, his non-threatening demeanor has served him well. He takes on the persona—or is it a patina?—of a kind of prairie sage.

***Opposite:** Harkness n.d. Rural Prototypes/Organization. Studies of vernacular forms from the agrarian Midwestern landscape*

A Landscape in Evolution

Brenda J. Brown

In his 1970 MLA thesis, *A Landscape in Evolution: The Graphic History of Champaign and Piatt Counties from 70,000 BC to AD 1860*, after citing J.B. Jackson, May Watts, John Muir, and Henry David Thoreau as exemplary readers of landscape, Terry Harkness stated his hypothesis:

> [A] pictorial-image format of "reading a regional landscape" can be a more efficient, more meaningful and more powerful way to understanding than an equivalent written exposition on the same subject. (3)

I first became aware of this document in a seminar with Bob Riley who admiringly used some of its pictures while lecturing on the evolution of Illinois's vernacular landscape. Later, cozy in the old Mumford Hall Library, I pored through its pages, awestruck by the thesis's scope. Looking at it now I am of two minds. Perhaps the dominant perspective is that of a former student, who encountered Terry twenty-some years after the thesis was finished and who watched his work continue to develop. Yet now I myself advise and evaluate graduate students on theses and practicums so I have a teacher's perspective as well.

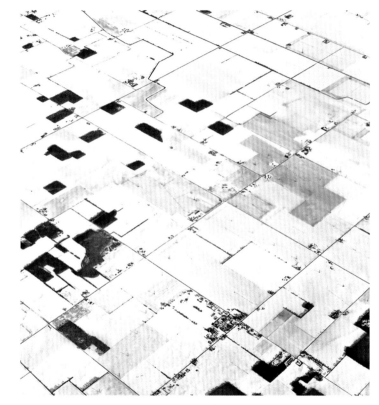

I still cannot help but be struck by the project's ambition, the somewhat foolhardy intention to tell a largely pictorial 70,000-year history of two Illinois counties. Actually, the original intention was to encompass 110 years more, to extend past the 1860 endpoint to the time of the writing. The many, many drawings are clear, if (as with some of the people and animals) occasionally clumsy. I am also impressed by what a very good student this is, at how he musters and displays so many of the tools and skills gained in his studies to analyze and interpret this Midwestern chunk of earth. And what a strong will this document's creator must have had! Indeed, in his support for Terry's 2007 Jot Carpenter nomination, Bob Riley recalled: "His enthusiasm and innovation made waves here when he was still a student. The Graduate College had to change its Masters thesis format requirements to handle his running text with sketch sidebars." And he added, "This is still the best introduction to the Central Illinois landscape around."

Above: Delicate Hold (photo courtesy of Ken McCown, December 2010)

Opposite: Sycamore with Red Winged Blackbird. Portrait of regional landscape character (photo courtesy of Ken McCown, March 2012)

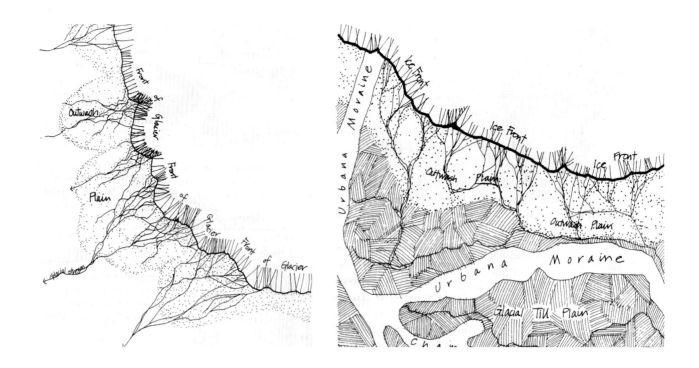

Above from left: Harkness, A Landscape in Evolution (1970, 16 and 35). Plan View of Outwash Plain (after Lamar and Williams, 1958) Bloomington Glacial Outwash (after anonymous, 1957)

As a student I sometimes marveled at the depth and breadth of Terry's knowledge of the Illinois landscape. Odd, in retrospect, that I did not then seriously consider how he acquired it. Surely much of his understanding must have come with this thesis. The document is not simply the fruits of his research, a presentation; it is an artifact of his investigations, of his own efforts to read and interpret a regional landscape through drawing. And this research both presaged and shaped the investigations that followed.

With stark clarity, Terry stated his intention to read the landscape in his own way—a reading grounded in drawing. Further, in the thesis conclusion, he sketched out a framework for his investigations to come.

> Growing out of this attempt at portraying landscape perception was the belief that there may be a natural basis for indigenous local or regional design. By starting out with the basic physical character and limitations of the regional landscape and adding the viable cultural components, a basis may emerge for regional, local and site design. (196)

Even more explicitly, Terry pointed to his techniques for "graphically transferring analysis and interpretation to others," e.g. contrasting and juxtaposing images to compare one factor (for example forest cover) in different times; comparing different factors (for example, forest cover, prairies, and wetlands) in one time; and using images and related texts as proximate interpretive partners.

Though Terry must have been around 30 in early 1970, it is tempting here to recall Wordsworth's assertion that the child is the father of the man, and to claim that the thesis holds all that was to come. However, this might be misleading. Most obviously, Terry did not actually design a landscape for his thesis, even though it sets up his designs for the next 40+ years. The projects for which I know Terry best—the sequence of Illinois gardens (one of which was part of the landmark *Transforming the American Garden* exhibition in 1986); the Foothill Mountain Observatory in Los Angeles County, California; the corporate campus in Fargo, North Dakota—all are informed by similar study and immersion in the regional landscape. Employing the techniques his thesis articulated, these projects' largely pictorial analyses and interpretive "readings" of landscape nature and culture are integral to these designs' presentation as well as to the designs themselves. There is no doubt these techniques are one reason why Terry has become well known even though most of these landscapes have never been built.

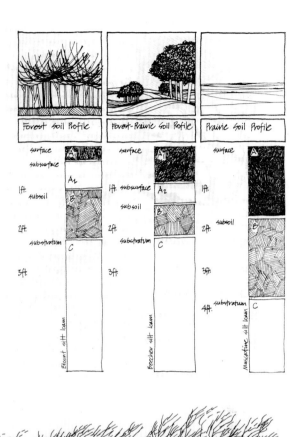

While continuities between the thesis and Terry's later works are apparent, so too are refinements. The drawings are always direct; there is a graphic clarity and simplicity and a reliance on line. Yet if one compares the thesis drawings with those for the Illinois gardens 20+ years on, it is clear that these later drawings—like the ones that followed—are more spare, more focused, more direct. They reflect more close observations of landscapes *en pleine aire*. If less bold than the thesis drawings, they are also more knowing of what will serve the design and its story; they are more elegant.

As time went on Terry used color more—"people love color" he once told me—felt-tip on Mylar especially, yet the line-work style along with the analytical techniques of his thesis are clearly discernable. The consideration of the cultural landscape post-1860, missing in the thesis, is also readily apparent in his later work. And of course there is the transmutation of the "reading" into an interpretive design response.

Above from top: Harkness, A Landscape in Evolution (1970, 45); Vegetation as a Factor in Soil Genesis. Terry Harkness, ca 1986. Detail from an East Central Illinois Garden

Today in North American MLA programs, though the requirement for a thesis or practicum has become more rare it has not disappeared. I think sometimes of having my students look at Terry's thesis, partly so they might marvel at the talent, energy, and ambition embodied in a nearly 50-year-old document, partly so they might simply learn from its form and content. But maybe most because I would like them to glimpse how such an endeavor can, if not change your life, then focus a lifelong enquiry.

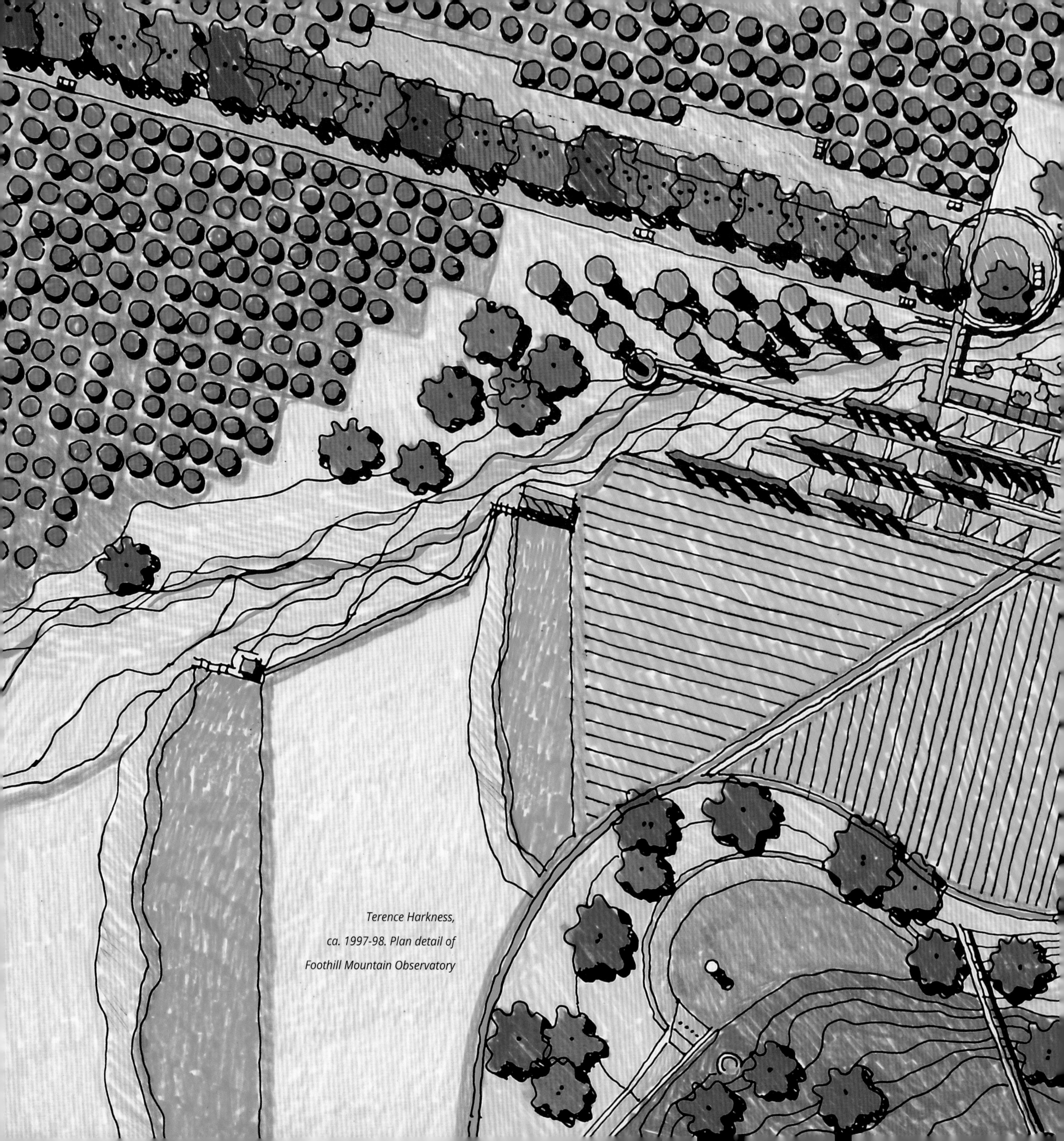

Terence Harkness,
ca. 1997-98. Plan detail of
Foothill Mountain Observatory

Portfolio

The Thinness of Things:
Illinois Gardens

Douglas Johnston

To most viewers of the East Central Illinois landscape, the predominant image is flatness. And openness. The post-glacial wind-deposited loess soils have blanketed any underlying topography with tens and even hundreds of feet of leveling soil. Caught between prairie fires and agricultural practices, the forests of the east gave way to vast regions of herbaceous materials. Depending on the time of year and whether you are sitting or standing, this extraordinary landscape leads to expansive vistas of earth and sky and immersion (historically) in a dense thicket of prairie grasses or (since the turn of the 20th century) corn. What dominates the view is that infinitesimally thin line that separates the land from the sky—the horizon.

Human settlement of East Central Illinois came relatively slowly thanks to the water-saturated, wind-blown landscape and its dense biomass. The use of drain tiling, developed back east but essential to the Midwest, permitted the development of agricultural livelihoods even at the well-documented expense of prairie and wetland. Water drained by tiles has to have some place to flow and the construction of drainways contributed a regularized pattern of incisions into the earth. To deflect the persistent winds, hedgerows provided shelter for fragile crops and farmsteads. To move goods to markets during all seasons, roads were elevated on embankments to maintain a drier surface.

Above: *Ditch (photo courtesy of Ken McCown, March 2012)*

Opposite: *Five Trees. Agrarian patterns of the central Illinois landscape (photo courtesy of Ken McCown, March 2012)*

But the Jeffersonian efficiency of the Northwest Ordinance grid drove the patterns of settlement and transformation at least as much as the character of the land itself. Divisions of land were framed by roads in mile grids, and farms and fields divided in halves and quarters—from 640, 320, 160, to 40 acres—a system of sectioning uniformly applied without favoritism or class privilege. The rhythms and markings of this uniquely American economy have been permanently imprinted into the land and our cultural imagination. That imagination is often communicated as flat or boring when compared to the northeast forests or mountains of the west. But all places possess powerful historical narratives and thus deserve our attention.

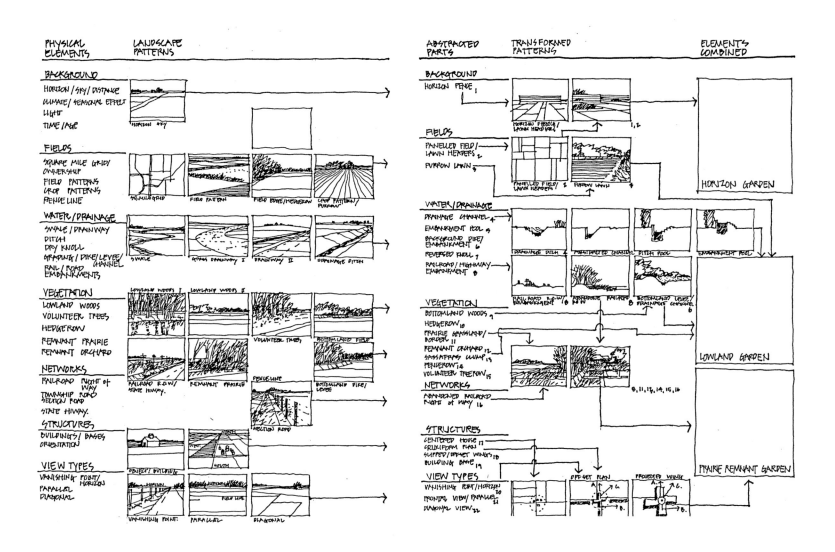

Terry Harkness, a keen and careful observer of the landscape, sees much more in the apparent plainness of the Illinois landscape. He sees the landscape not as a recipient of imported design forms but as a source of unique form, literally grounded in its place. Harkness's designs for east-central Illinois are not based on conventions of what the landscape should be, but a celebration of what the landscape is. Abstracted and magnified, fields and groves become geometric planes. Where roads and hedgerows border the fields, insertions of edges mark the planes on the ground while hedges and fences frame them. Channels and roads are the figurative and literal expressions of drainage and movement with the horizon separating or joining the earth and sky.

Above: Terry Harkness, n.d. Analysis of landscape elements, patterns, abstraction, and transformation for An East Central Illinois Garden

Opposite: Strays and Shadows, the agrarian patterns of the central Illinois landscape (photo courtesy of Ken McCown, August 2009)

Above clockwise from left: The *Workingman's Garden. Terry Harkness and Doug Johnston, ca. 1993. Site Plan for 716 Prairie Avenue; Terry Harkness and Doug Johnston, ca. 1993. (photos courtesy of Doug Johnston)*

The Workingman's Garden (ca. 1994). Harkness's work transforms and reinterprets the common landscape, so common as to become invisible to most eyes. Harkness's perspective (pun intended) is visible in many of his designed landscapes and felt especially strongly in "The Workingman's (Workers) Garden." The Worker's Garden is a realized design situated in a residential lot in Champaign, Illinois. Because the house is a classic 1920s Craftsman bungalow, the framing concept for the landscape was to draw from gardens of that period that provided utilitarian, recreational and aesthetic roles without much separation between them: the household vegetable garden, the drying yard, the play area, etc. These programmatic elements were transferred or reinterpreted into a modern Craftsman garden, preserving the vegetable gardens and play spaces, while substituting other functions and forms for the drying yard and cistern.

Interview with Molly Briggs and M. Elen Deming, August 1, 2011:

TGH: "Doug Johnston's garden is what we call The Worker's Garden. ... a real place, built for thirty-five hundred dollars and all his labor. ... We'd sit over at Bevier [Hall] and we'd doodle, we'd work it out on napkins and then he'd go home and build it. That's how it happened. And what's interesting about it is that it has that kind of clarity. We [wondered]: "is it possible to design a wonderful residential garden for $3500?" We submitted it on a lark to the state [ASLA] chapter awards and we got an Honor Award. Because everything getting awards were these incredibly expensive projects on the North Shore of Chicago. So we [submitted] just for the fun of it."

The lot—front, sides, and back—were designed as subdivided flat fields marked by headers around the perimeters. An evergreen hedge marks the northern side of the property and a hedgerow of upright maples stretches from the street to the back of the deep, narrow lot. Two panels of native prairie grasses and forbs line the south side of the lot in front and jump to the north side against the hedge in the back. A small panel of turf extends the house toward the street, and a larger panel of grass in the back serves as an all-purpose play space. A walk connects the house to a water tank/fountain structure set at the rear of the property. The simple rectilinear forms create a formal order. Use of basic materials—wood, gravel, concrete—avoids pretension. This is a garden that is of its region with pleasure and utility blended into one. It is familiar at the same time it is unique.

Below and following page: Terry Harkness. Formative details and plan of An East Central Illinois Garden (1986).

An East Central Illinois Garden (1984-1986).

Harkness's working method involves years of iterative study, refining and testing a series of related parti. He constantly seeks opportunities to "test" his conceptual ideas and studies in material interventions. The most important testbeds include his own garden, of course, as well as the gardens of friends, for example the garden he designed for Jon and Judith Liebman (ca 1995). But as just one of an extended series of such material experiments, the Worker's Garden is heir to Harkness's mastery of formal concepts from scores of earlier conceptual studies from the 1980s. It is in this sense that we can say *An East Central Illinois Garden* was the beating heart of a conceptual project in search of its site(s). Like so many of his projects, its variations were painstakingly studied, sketched, revised, and redrawn many times over several years. It also represents the first iconic design for which Terry Harkness is now justifiably admired.

In 1986, *An East Central Illinois Garden* received national recognition when it was featured in Michael Van Valkenburgh's exhibition and subsequent catalog *Transforming the American Garden* (Harvard Graduate School of Design). Below are excerpts from previously published essays explaining Harkness's working methods and design intentions in his own words.

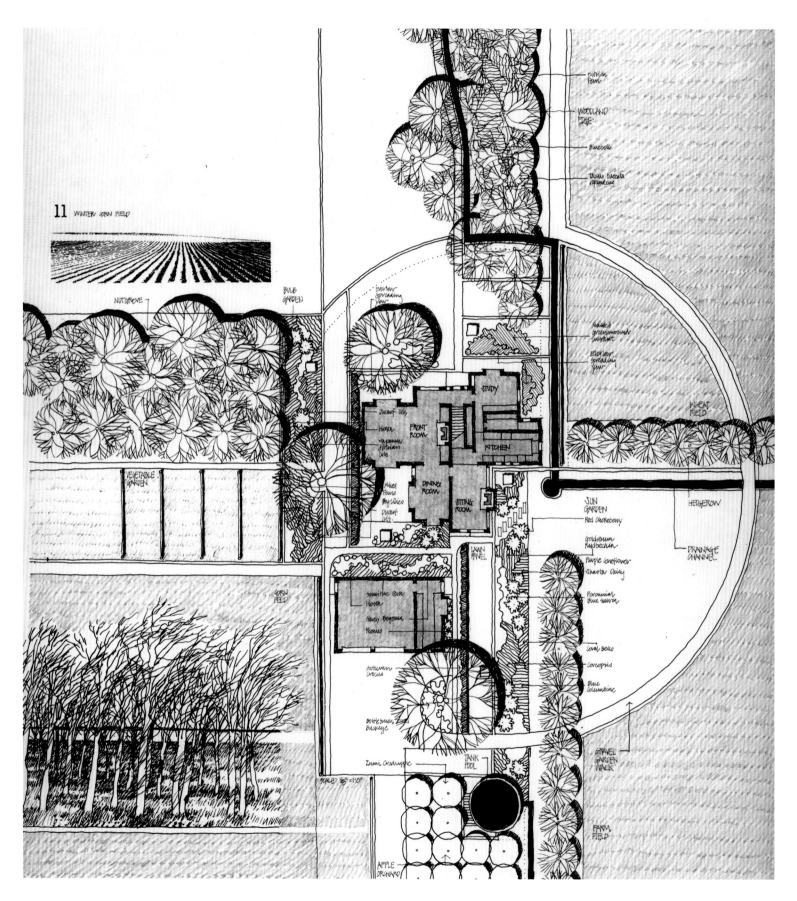

11 WINTER CORN FIELD

NUT GROVE

BULB GARDEN

VEGETABLE GARDEN

CORN FIELD

ostrich fern

WOODLAND EDGE

bluebells

Taxus baccata repandens

Everlow Spreading Yew

dwarf gold mound currant

Everlow Spreading Yew

WHEAT FIELD

STUDY

dwarf fig

Hosta

FRONT ROOM

KITCHEN

Japanese Siberian Iris

Mixed Ferns Bay Laurel Dwarf Fig

DINING ROOM

SITTING ROOM

HEDGEROW

SUN GARDEN
Red Chokeberry

Goldsturm Rudbeckia

Purple Coneflower

Shasta Daisy

Perennial Blue Salvia

DRAINAGE CHANNEL

LAWN PANEL

Sensitive Fern Hosta

Hardy Begonia Peonies

Coral Bells

Coreopsis

Blue Columbine

Autumn Crocus

Bottlebrush Buckeye

GRAVEL GARDEN WALK

Zumi Crabapple

TANK POOL

FARM FIELD

SCALE: 1/16" = 1'0"

APPLE ORCHARD

As Harkness puts it, the work "reflects my preoccupation with the visual qualities of [the rural Middle West] and my attempt to conform and reveal them to others." In his 1986 essay "An East Central Illinois Garden," he lucidly explains his attachment:

> Living in the Middle West and experiencing its particular light, the expanse of sky and horizon, and the effect of sunset on the flat plane of farm lands—these have been particularly powerful components of my visual sense. During the summer, impressions of changing field patterns have provided experience in spaciousness, incised pattern and exploration. Such experiences have enhanced my visual sense of the power and friendliness of this distinctive landscape.
>
> ...
>
> There are other important qualities present in the landscape of East Central Illinois: the richness and detail of winter trees, for example, seen against the sky. Ground fog of late fall shrouds the intermittent lines of hedgerows. The aspect of age and its effects are revealed in trees and structures: the visual quality of growth originally controlled and confined, but now aging or escaping ... There is a congruence between the landscape and the independent, practical farmers who live there. The unadorned quality of plain concrete, metal grain bins and white clapboard siding bespeak an austerity and functional practicality that is visually direct and uncompromising—utilitarian in its economy, austere in its directness.

Below left to right: Terry Harkness, n.d. Horizon Garden, Lowland Garden, and Remnant Prairie Garden

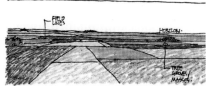

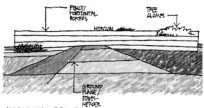

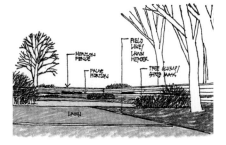

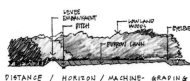

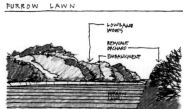

This garden's purpose is to reflect these characteristics as a visible, built expression, to be experienced through time, seasons and changing light. A change of climate such as the dusting and drifting of dry snow should reveal the region's winds and the variability of the continental climate. The temporary flooding of the front lawn during and after a summer storm should invite barefoot wading. The garden focuses on and celebrates the landscape; it should demonstrate the power and qualities of this unique place. The design sources for this garden are in the landscape itself. The garden and the landscape are inseparable (*Places* vol 3:3, 6).

Interview with Molly Briggs, August 8, 2011:

TGH: "The water starts here, and it goes all the way around. So this is actually a grain storage bin that's above ground—a swimming tank. When you're in the tank, it's 10 or 15 feet above the ground and it's flat and you're in water. How wonderful is that? I mean, how wonderful is that?! I remember growing up as a kid, I went to a relative's farm and they had a tank like that, an old wooden water tank and we'd climb up there and swim and we could look out. We could see the whole countryside. So what this is about is, you see this one way on the ground as you move around, but when you go across it, whoa! All of a sudden it rains and it fills up, and the water moves through and it goes over the spillway; when it goes over this then you get this whole different understanding of water, flatness, elevation, and drainage. So there's a whole bunch of things you're trying to do. This tells you how to extend the notion of being in the building and seeing out, being in the garden and being in the landscape.

So there [are] these three pathways, or visual ensembles, or scales; and the water or the grid leads you out, or moves you through it, or across it or along its edge. In this case you're following the water through the grove, and so this is actually a concrete path that you go along like this, and so each of these, the seasonality I used to see when I was a kid, visiting here; you'd get a summer rain, and you'd get a puddle that would fill up in a lawn, and we'd go play in it, go lay in it, and then it'd dry up. So all of a sudden the immediacy of rainfall and how it flows, gathers, stores—wow!

MCB: "I want to make sure I understand right, that this is about making the landscape itself readable, making the larger landscape readable in this design."

TGH: "Right. And the point about this is it starts with memory and experience. It would go here. It would be here or here. And then it would go to experience. And then it goes to making place, where you actually do the place stuff. It all feeds down to this, the places that you made or the places within the places you made. ... It doesn't matter the name of the experience, there just needs to be a richness about it.

Although the East Central Illinois Garden itself remains a purely conceptual project, it has been tested repeatedly for different scales and sites. For instance, *A Suburban Garden* is an interpretation of the original scaled down to a site comprising four conventional lots. And many key elements and principles have found their way into other realized gardens including Terry's own garden (i.e. the Horizon Garden, and the Gelvin Garden at the Krannert Art Museum, University of Illinois Urbana-Champaign (Deming and Harleman 94-99).

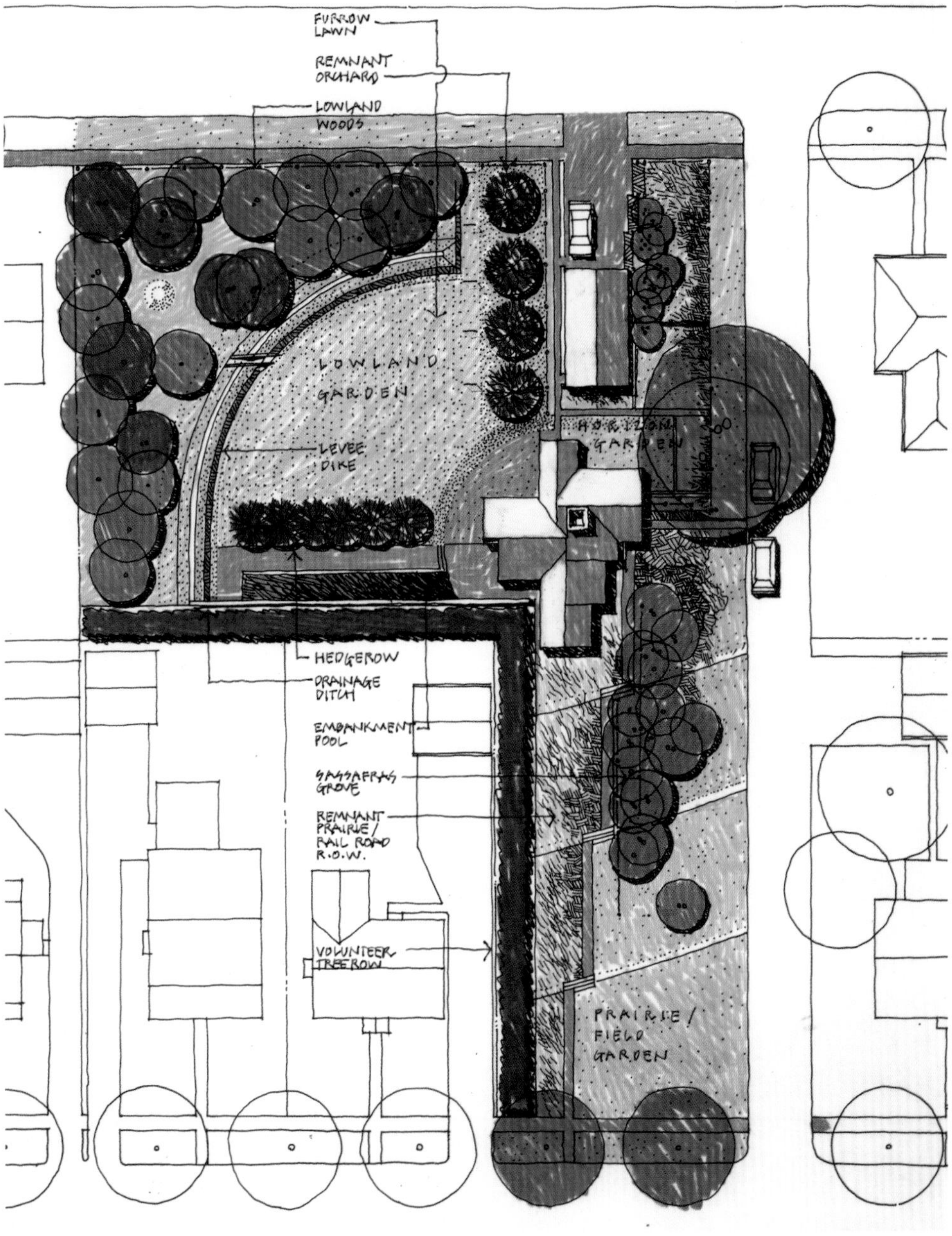
FURROW LAWN
REMNANT ORCHARD
LOWLAND WOODS
LOWLAND GARDEN
LEVEE DIKE
HORIZON GARDEN
HEDGEROW
DRAINAGE DITCH
EMBANKMENT POOL
SASSAFRAS GROVE
REMNANT PRAIRIE/ RAIL ROAD R.O.W.
VOLUNTEER TREEROW
PRAIRIE/ FIELD GARDEN

Left: *Terry Harkness, n.d. Site plan for A Suburban Garden (site adapted from Harkness's own home and garden in Champaign, IL)*

Too often, garden designs have a sameness originating in ideas developed for another time or place. Terry Harkness's designs have an authenticity and elegance grounded in their place. His work is always original, crafted by a discerning eye that delights in bringing out the beauty in things most of us overlook. His gift is to find the poetry in common landscapes all around us—and to distill the essential qualities and flavors and elements that distinguish them from anywhere else in the world.

Foothill Mountain Observatory

Ken McCown

How We Choose to Dwell. Landscape architects often say they are 'generalists.' At their worst, generalists in landscape architecture merely offer palliative care to anodyne real estate development. When they are at their best, however, I like to call them 'integrative specialists.' As integrative specialists, the core competencies for landscape architects include site analysis combined with good planning and design responding to the analysis.

Competent designs and plans demonstrate a basic integration of urban and natural elements. To integrate a program into a site and incur as little damage as possible is the least a landscape architect should do. To make a site sustainable, or perhaps regenerative, is an even more sophisticated means of integrating urban and natural systems.

Landscape performance requires understanding a dynamic confluence of systems to harmonize a place within its larger context. Performative hybrid systems on a site may require interpretive signage to help people understand how regenerative landscapes work. But because people need to live with the understanding of how their places work culturally and ecologically, still more integration is necessary from the specialist. Their relationship to place should be like a marriage—not merely sustainable, but also nurturing, co-evolving, aiming at growth. When elements, systems, and people are integrated skillfully through planning and design, an ecologically literate culture may take root and develop.

Foothill Mountain Observatory is a purely conceptual design intended as a place where people may come to understand the natural and cultural evolution of California. The Observatory instantiates the polemic that landscapes matter to culture. Perhaps more important, it suggests how people may gain ecological literacy by experiencing thoughtful design and planning.

Above: Harkness, n.d. Geomorphological study; deposition and alluvial fan in San Gabriel Mountains

Opposite: Los Angeles against the mountains (photo courtesy of Ken McCown, April 2017)

> *Interview with Molly Briggs, July 25, 2011:*
>
> *MCB: Wasn't [Foothill Mountain] also described as an Observatory? Where does the word observatory come in?*
>
> *TGH: Because that's what I decided. It wasn't meant to be a park or garden. Observatories are instruments to understand the world. And so the park or the garden is an instrument to understand the natural and cultural process of Southern California and water. As one of the reviewers said ... "Gosh, I can go to this one place and I can understand the whole water history of Southern California!" And that wasn't my objective when I was starting out,*

I had a much more personal thing I was chasing after; but she's absolutely right. You could go to the garden and you could see every era or process of how water was managed or aqua-mined or captured. And so an observatory really is the right word to me, because it allows you to see the world and understand the world; it creates frames by which to measure change.

Foothill Mountain Observatory marries *ukiyo-e* prints of views of Mt. Fuji and the Tokaido Road with John McPhee's *The Control of Nature* (1989) and, from them both, creates an idea about how to design for place-making. During a period of disharmony among the classes in Japan, the emperor commissioned Hokusai to prepare the *Thirty-Six Views of Mt. Fuji* to remind the Japanese people of their culture. The views showed people in various activities of daily life, engaged in their markets, industries, rituals, and agriculture. The prints also depict seasonal changes in the landscape. Mt. Fuji is ever-present—sometimes snow-covered, sometimes with just a snowcap; in some the mountain is brightly colored, suggesting autumn or a tectonic event about to occur. By showing Japanese island culture integrated into nature's rhythms, the artist highlights indexical changes in the landscape. Urban and rural, natural and infrastructural scenes were all depicted in the same way. None of them were romanticized, or privileged against the other—the prints show people living harmoniously in towns and within nature. The message was that landscape was the foundation of the Japanese culture and all people shared it.

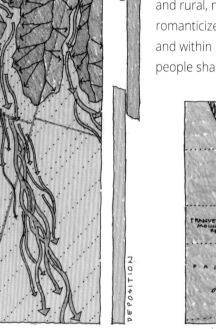

Thirty-Six Views of Mt. Fuji offers just one example of how visual art may incite the idea that landscape matters to culture. Similarly, John McPhee's *The Control of Nature* (1989) reveals the importance of infrastructure (the prefix "infra" meaning below or unseen) through his literary art. Mr. McPhee uses three places, including the Los Angeles metro, to reveal how our static Western ideas about occupying places conflict with the dynamics of landscape. Infrastructure is the focus for his book—what happens when flooding, debris, fire, and earthquakes threaten settlements? Are we thinking about how we settle our places in the right way? Mr. McPhee's writings directly inspire the Foothill Mountain Observatory inquiry.

If Mr. Harkness's midwestern gardens were an opportunity to explore *if* landscape means, his Observatory demonstrates that landscapes matter. Now a nearly native resident of the Midwest, Mr. Harkness grew up in Southern California, witness to the greatest changes the region has ever seen. The Observatory project was his recollection of a complex set of relationships that led to rapid changes in Federal and State policy, engineered infrastructure, disaster management, agricultural transitions, real estate, and culture—each playing a role in creating new patterns and forms, and often erasing the past. The design of Foothill Mountain Observatory thus demonstrates the potential of landscape architects to be 'integrative specialists,' presenting landscape dynamics instead of representing static forms.

Interview with Molly Briggs and M. Elen Deming, August 1, 2011:

MED: There is a lexicon, a formal vocabulary that derives from the cultural and natural history of this place, from which you build a new syntax. Typology seems to be a key theme driving through your work. And that is strongly evident in both the East Central Illinois Garden and the Foothill Mountain Observatory. Do you think it's true of other work as well, either before or after?

TGH: Oh absolutely. But I'll throw a caveat in there, and this is why I love the Foothill Mountain Observatory. Both of these places have meant so much to me personally. ... The Foothill Mountain Observatory is about where I grew up and it's about understanding the processes—social and cultural, the formal vocabularies, all of the things that make up California's landscape. California is richly complex, and the Observatory [shows us] that ... it integrates not only the cultural and the natural but [also] my affinity for historic landscapes and the geometries that I've derived from those that really are important to me ...

I realized after doing a project once where I tried to be rational about it, where it was a rational design, it was lifeless. It was just totally lifeless. It didn't have any kind of feeling or experience to it. So one of the things I've tried never to do, is never to impose a geometry before I understand what the problem is or what's going on. I just let it come by itself, the ordering of it.

What's interesting about the Foothill Mountain Observatory is it's very much like Dan Kiley, in terms of his love of Le Notre and his geometries. Foothill Mountain Observatory uses French geometries in this incredibly uneven landscape. Like those two gardens in Paris ... Parc du Sceaux is one and then [St. Cloud]—these are in really varied topography. ... But when you lay French geometry, which is axial and about planes and edges, on uneven topography, you get the most wonderful things to happen. ... They're fractured. And that's what I love; in retrospect that's what happens in the Foothill Mountain Observatory. It's not a symmetrical balance; yes, it starts off with geometry, as axial things going in various directions, but all the stuff that you're highlighting is very organic stuff ... organic natural systems. But you're holding it still with the garden geometry, the park geometry, the Observatory geometry laid over it. You move above it and along its edges at different elevations. So you can see it all, and it holds it still, while all this dynamic of earth, mountain building, and wasting—all this stuff is happening so you can see it. The design holds it still.

Above: *Dam holding back the San Gabriel Mountains (photo courtesy of Ken McCown, April 2017)*

Opposite: *Harkness, n.d. (ca. 1996-97) Geomorphological studies. Analysis of tectonic shifts and erosion/mass movement patterns in southern California*

The Design of Foothill Mountain Observatory

One of the most overlooked aspects of place design is the position of the viewer, their movement, and experience. Mr. Harkness spent quite a bit of time searching for the observatory site. He found a place with all of the elements he needed that would let him tell a comprehensive story of the natural and cultural landscape of the Los Angeles metropolitan area. So, how does one design in order to integrate people with places? In the Observatory's axial circulation system, Mr. Harkness demonstrates the use of position and place to thread people into a powerful sequential experience of the richness of Southern California.

Mr. Harkness brings the visitor to the site along the grid lines of the National Land Ordinance of 1785. He registers the visitor along a straight eucalyptus-lined road, reminiscent of the entrances of many old farms in the region. The road frames the view of the mountains and abruptly ends due to the dramatic upward shift in topography. At the road end, visitors traverse a wash ripping through the western side of the site, an index of annual flooding. The bridge is a common infrastructure encountered by Southern Californians, which Mr. Harkness noted in his design intention—to start people with an experience they would find familiar. In the master plan for Foothill Mountain Observatory, he counterposes a natural, unmanaged wash in contrast to the managed wash on the opposite side of the site from the entry.

Left to right from top: *TGH. n.d. Perspective sketch of two water management systems; compare to footbridge over outwash canyon (photo courtesy of Ken McCown, April 2017); Harkness, n.d. Sketches for water conservation management head house and detail for irrigation overlook; Sketch of dryland botanical specimen inspired by the Huntington Botanical Gardens, Pasadena*

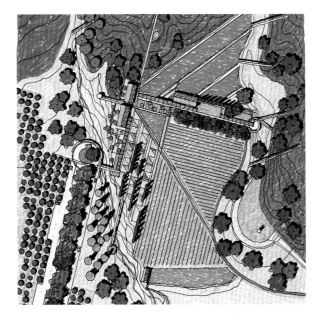

The orthogonal grid of the Land Ordinance forms the two main spines of the design. The visitor may move along the north-south line up into the mountains on a stair to see and learn the complexities of the plant communities. This trip up the mountains also lets the visitor learn about ecological disturbances of fire and flood, and reveals the management of these disturbances through firebreaks and water retention. An emergency storage drum anchors the north end of this axis in the foothills.

The other spine aligns itself with the mountain range, allowing people to see the rising sides of the range tapering into the distance of the Los Angeles basin. Cultural landscapes from different eras and land use types surround this spine. This area tells a story of how water use dictates landscape design style throughout the basin. A walk through this area reveals xeric landscapes of contemporary residential land uses, lush plantings in higher irrigation zones, and agricultural landscapes consisting of crops as well as vineyards.

At the east end of this east-west circulation spine is an overlook to a retention module, which enables the visitor to see the managed landscape. A dam bounding a colossal basin collects mud and rock debris from annual floods. This is an engineered landscape but just as dynamic as a natural one. This area is similar to basins all along the foothills that protect Los Angeles from debris destruction during flooding. These basins fill to the top with rock during major storms and then must be emptied of debris afterwards. What a dramatic change in the Observatory, from a fifty-foot-deep basin when empty, to being flush with the surrounding grade by captured rocks, sand, and mud after rains.

Above: Harkness, n.d. (ca. 1996-97). Plan detail of Foothill Mountain Observatory

Opposite: Harkness, n.d. (ca 1996-97). Foothill Mountain Observatory concept for development of landscape typology

To the south end of the site is the spillway and baustrocephinian water recharge system, commonly used in Southern California to replenish groundwater. Water moves down the alluvial fan into spreading fields. These shallow and broad ponds are a magnet for birds along the Pacific Flyway. Visitors would see this intercontinental avian ecological system. Mr. Harkness positions the viewer to stand north of the spreading fields. With the sun to the south, the water would appear golden and opaque from the sunlight, a distinctly different view than the other rugged and rocky parts of the Observatory.

A trip along the two spines in the design reveals Southern California agriculture, geology, engineering, culture, ecology, and other factors integrated into the observatory site. The compositional qualities of how the design fits into the local and regional landscape show the potential capacities of the landscape architect to integrate people with their place by letting them see their culture through the Earth's systems and responses to them. The circulation systems provide the viewers with the maximum "combined total impact" by integrating distant views into the

Observatory site to tell the complex stories of the landscape. Given the dynamics of this world of materials in motion, as Mr. Harkness suggests, "the design holds it still" at least long enough to perceive their patterns.

The Observatory project embraces the complex conditions of landscape through design, not interpretation or metaphor. The observatory is not a representation of regionalism through design, it is a framework of circulation and program to integrate people with natural systems, agriculture, and infrastructure. The design helps recalibrate people to their landscapes, not as nature, or garden, or infrastructure, but as an integrated whole of elements and systems evolving over time to shape and reflect culture.

Interview with Molly Briggs and M. Elen Deming, August 1, 2011:

TGH: It took me forever to figure out what was going on! This is the world I grew up in, right here. ... north of San Bernadino. Those are the alluvial outwash plains and these are eucalyptus and this area was all orchards, down below. ... And this whole agricultural type changed in ten years! Before that they tried to do it with dried fruits because they couldn't do it with fresh fruits [but] when they finally could put ice in cars, refrigerated cars, this worked. This is a story about climate and water. You can grow anything if you can get water to it. That was true then and that's true today! And here are the suburbs creeping up that hill. [Foothill Mountain Observatory] tells that whole story, about mountain building and wasting...

John McPhee wrote about this, he wrote the story of all this mountain building and erosion and destruction and flooding. That is the story of this garden. Look at the axis. It goes right up the mountain, on a cross-axis, and then there are all of these terraces that come off. There you see going up to the two canyons on either side. One is unchanged; the other has been harnessed. So this brown teardrop shape on the right hand corner collects the boulder and debris from these flash floods. The green trapezoids are actually recharging all the water that comes off and you distribute it through these basins ... The left stays as it is, the right is managed. You don't see the water in the wet season. You get all these braided streams coming out.

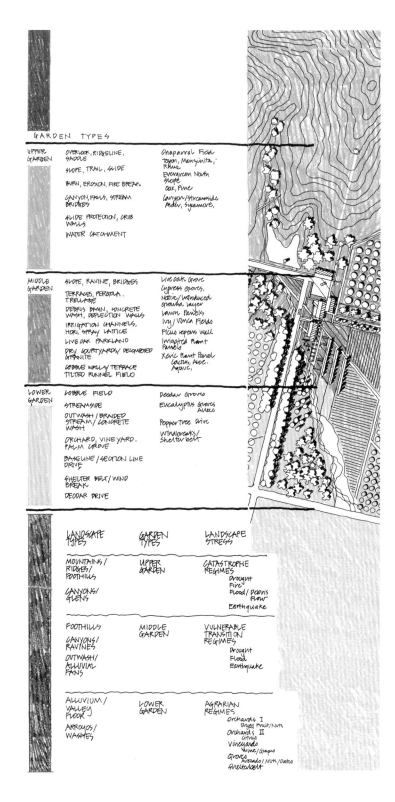

So this device, this Observatory, is designed to capture each of the vegetation communities, each of the agricultural communities, each of the water management communities. It takes you above them. ... The whole idea is that by car, bridge, on foot, ramp, or staircase you go through every one of these zones, and you climb up the side of a mountain. This is looking back down. So all the prototypes are there, all the vegetative communities that would grow in that place. ... This shows where these two landscapes [cultural and natural; managed and spontaneous] meet. Mountains are going up and wasting and it all happens there at that intersection.

And so, here are the precedents. How are we going to walk up the side of the mountain? That's how. Split face boulders. The design strategies. The steps are down here too. That's the vocabulary. You can see how it works. We were talking about how you understand the world. One way you're climbing up and looking back to the Santa Catalina and the ocean, but the other experience is you're looking left and right and the sun comes up to the right and then sets to the far left. There's this whole orientation of the site.

...I did all the research: if this is where it's eroding, where is all the mass going to? The tan is the alluvial fan, the rusty red is the mountains and it shows all the flow. You can see if there's a storm up there with three or four inches in a few hours, how fast is that going to come down? ... One day I went up under the freeway and around the corner and I couldn't hear any cars. But I heard this funny sound like sand falling. What is that? It was all this material just running down because the slope of the mountain is steeper than the natural angle of repose. ... The mountains are actually growing, among the fastest tectonic activity on Earth. The mountains are rising faster than they're eroding! You actually see it coming down. They get boulders the size of Volkswagens. It comes down as slurry with big boulders. The heavier material drops first. That's what it looks like in one of those canyons. I realized—how do you tell that story? These people are living in this place; do they have a clue? They do, but they don't. I tried to figure out how to capture that. So that's the story of two canyons, left and right. One has been managed, one has been left as it is.

Landscapes Matter

The essay on the Foothill Mountain Observatory that Terry Harkness wrote for the Eco-revelatory catalog (*Landscape Journal*, 1998) features a line from a poem by N. Scott Momaday called "The Earth." The quote incites people to immerse themselves in their landscapes—an appeal to intimately understand the places in which we dwell. Today, twenty years after Foothill Mountain Observatory was first published, the end of the poem is perhaps even more compelling: "For we are held by more than the force of gravity to the earth. It is the entity from which we are sprung, and that into which we are dissolved in time. The blood of the whole human race is invested in it."

With increasing urbanization and the bulk of humanity growing up in metropolitan areas away from landscapes and supported by infrastructure, we need observatories to help people see, appreciate, and invest in landscapes. And there should be more than investment. While Terry Harkness was growing up in the Los Angeles area, Richard Neutra rose to international prominence. Neutra's book *Survival Through Design* argued passionately that, even in the face of urbanization and industrialization, people might be linked to nature through architecture. Similarly, the Foothill Mountain Observatory is a personal passion project, a call for landscape architects to use design to link people to their changing landscapes. Both for Neutra and Harkness, the question is not how to create geometry in design, it is how to use that geometry to solve the problem of integrating people into the rhythms of the world. People need intimate and nurturing relationships to places. Foothill Mountain Observatory is a plea for people to come to know their landscapes through a more meaningful relationship.

Above: *In Wash Up to San Gabriel Mountains (photo courtesy of Ken McCown, April 2017)*

Opposite: *Terry Harkness and Ken McCown (ca. 1998). Foothill Mountain Observatory exhibition model*

Taj Mahal Cultural Heritage District

By Amita Sinha

At the University of Illinois in 2000, Terry Harkness worked with a team of faculty and students to develop the master plan for the Taj Mahal Cultural Heritage District. The plan was commissioned by the Uttar Pradesh Tourism Department and presented to them as well as many other local institutions in the city of Agra. So far, it has been implemented only on a short stretch between the two World Heritage Sites of Taj Mahal and Agra Fort on the Yamuna riverfront. However the development plan remains an important blueprint for the state as it seeks to expand the scope of conservation from the historic monument and its garden to the larger landscape. In this endeavor Terry's way of seeing played a pivotal role in visualizing the riverfront as a heritage corridor.

Interview with Molly Briggs, August 8, 2011:

MCB: You talk about design that allows visitors or viewers to learn about a place on multiple levels, by looking and moving around and maybe also by talking to each other—as opposed to learning by more indirect means, like representations, some of which aren't even visual, like literature. But then there is a sentence, the last sentence in the article "Views of the Taj" (Landscape Journal 2009): "This [journey into the larger landscape] will convert the tourist into a traveler, not just in search of visual edification but one who seeks to know and understand the object of one's gaze" (215). I thought the article suggested how the gaze happens in space and also from a moving vantage point, a wonderful suggestion.

TGH: It's the magic of the place ... I was trying to show that idea, in just that sense you give it. This is the Red Fort, with an active military group in here, but here are the old parts of the fort, with gardens and fountains. There are three different places where you look out over all this. These are huge walls, and then there's the city. This is the view you have from here. They have this wonderful waterworks that is mentioned in [D.F. Ruggles, 2008, Islamic Gardens and Landscapes]. All this water was brought up from the river into here, and then it was brought in to water the fountains. Which is just like France, with all the waterworks. ... This is the most fantastic thing.

...[A]nd this is where the maintenance people lived and the nursery where they grow the plants to replant is in here. This story in itself is fabulous. This used to be a community—the same 900 by 900 feet—where the craftsmen who built this place lived. The taxes on the work they did after it was built paid for its maintenance. Now ... this area is really active and very vital. ... You can walk through all this.

This is the path that we made lower than this level but higher than this level. It had a seat wall that you could sit on, these certain points where you could stop. It also allowed the farmers to get down ... they have vegetable crops

Below: View of Taj Mahal from Yamuna River, looking south (photo courtesy of A. Sinha)

Opposite: Terry Harkness et al (2000). Plan drawing of Taj Mahal Cultural Heritage District

and there's buffalo and cattle in here, and the women would go down and do laundry. This is all in active use when it isn't flooded ... You can walk through all of this, you can walk through any part of contemporary life, plus you can put all these historic sites together. ... It's all there. This is about a 15 to 20-minute walk. ... It's just unbelievable.

Above: *Sketch of proposed visitor center across the river, viewing the Taj Mahal. Terry Harkness 2000*

Opposite clockwise from left:
Fifteen years after the study was completed, this view of Taj shows part of the Heritage District plan gardens to the north (photo courtesy of A. Sinha); Water jets and runnels in the chahar bagh of the Taj Mahal; Pilgrims folding laundry on the banks of the Yamuna River; View of Taj from over the conservation area along the Yamuna River, from the west

The whole notion was that if this is a garden that's still extant, and this is a shrine, and there's stuff along here; you can start to put it together. This just says what's going on, district-wise ... we were trying to figure out how do the clusters go, where are the hotels, what are the viewsheds? You put it all together. The high ground is here, the promenade is there, and then the river is down here. Even if it floods high it's what you call a hardened walkway and walls; it won't wash away.

We worked on it over there together. Three or four other faculty [Bellafiore, Orland, McCown, Sinha] were there. Fifteen students were there. ... The key was, and this appalled our hosts, we walked every square foot. And a large part of this was simply open latrine fields. There are no public or private restrooms. We insisted on seeing every part of it; we walked every bit of it.

What was interesting is that I had looked at it in the abstract, originally. ... I design everything ahead of time, before I know anything –

MCB: *Do you mean in your mind's eye?*

TGH: *Absolutely. Because then you go to a place, and you test it out. Does it change? It should change. You're always trying to figure out some abbreviated way to test—do you have the right knowledge, the right information? Do you need to talk to more people? Do you understand the problem? I've always been that way. I had an idea of what it ought to be. It was this big circular thing ... because it would tie it all together. ... at least this is what I was doodling on the airplane flying over. But when we get there, it's all stretched out along here. ... so you have to confirm it. We would talk, we would go out in the morning and visit all these places. They were just wonderful. In the afternoon we'd come back to the hotel and they had this small banquet room where we worked. We'd work all afternoon and evening. We did this for fifteen days. On the twelfth day we presented to people there, and then we presented again, and we went to New Delhi and presented a couple of times more. ... Then we came back [to Illinois] and spent a semester in the studio developing it [for publication]. In the summer the booklet, the master plan, came out. Then we went back [to India] and presented it again ... [so it could be] tested and confirmed.*

What and how did Terry see? In the week-long site workshop we held in Agra, Terry walked, observed, and sketched. In producing several key diagrams of landscape morphology, visual structure, and movement systems, he shared his understanding of the riverfront landscape to the team, which became the basis for planning and site design. Out in the field, and in the absence of GIS and Google Earth or any detailed survey of land and river hydrology, Terry's intuitive understanding of landscape structure, gleaned through walking and alert looking, was essential for the project to take shape. Terry's sketches rendered legible the connections between the flood plain, farmland, urban settlement, street network, and monument-gardens.

The confusion a visitor might usually experience in this chaotic landscape was gone; instead a hidden order, not visible to the naked eye, emerged. From among hundreds of photographs, Terry selected just a few for making detailed studies through drawing. As he drew the lines of bridges, monuments, roads, farm furrows, and the riverbank, the landscape structure became apparent— structure that could then be amplified and augmented through design.

Interview with Molly Briggs, August 15, 2011:

TGH: So there is this whole array of how the river and the landscape and the climate and the rulers envisioned and lived in it. The important thing was all the historic sites that are not just gardens and not just the Taj but this whole set of things around the river and ... all the land uses that knit it together. The United States National Park Service went and did their ... master plan, which was about the national park to the north, 350 acres, which we enlarged another 300 acres. So there's ... Ebba Koch's idea of the gardens; the reality of the historic sites; the place where the people who conquered the area came from; the monuments; then there was the whole of idea of the views of the Taj where we're trying to understand how all of this has become a heritage site, not only nationally but internationally. It's such an important part of Indian heritage. How do you make that available not just as one site but a multiplicity of sites?

... because it's travelers, it's certain kinds of imperial capital and the cultural capital; it's that connection, and it's also the connection of feudal and national consolidation. So you need to put all this together —you're trying to put the story together so that the tourists don't just go to one place for thirty minutes and run away. How do you think about that; and then keep all the living fabric, the neighborhood, the rural families, the foundries, the nursery businesses—how to do keep all that intact, and have this multiple overlay of visitation? That's the story that really engaged me. That story you got just by the immersion that we made the students go through ...

Interview with Molly Briggs, August 8, 2011:

TGH: The other key idea was the Views of Mt. Fuji series ... the idea that I was thinking about, from having been to Japan, was the Views of Mt. Fuji and the Tokkaido Road; of all the woodcuts.

MCB: as in, Hokusai?

TGH: Yes. From Edo to Kyoto—that to me was the germ. The cultural memory of Japan, that insular culture, and what those views meant. I had seen the book in Japan: Views From the Tokaido Road. Along the way was a set of stories. ... There was always some incident, some vivid story about a particular place. When I was in Japan studying, there was another book, a guide to Kyoto, where ... every garden in the book, let's say there were 25 gardens, had a little three- to four-page thing about its history—the context of the times. All of a sudden every garden—the Silver Pavilion—had a story that talked about the plague and what happened then, how the garden survived.

Brian Orland and I both said, that's what this is—except it's "Views of the Taj." It was that same set of ideas, the views of Fuji and the plan. We would go out and look and say, okay, what are the stories? Does it have to do with water supply? Agriculture? Does it have to do with the different kinds of economies? If you look at that plan, every part of that thing had a different economy, even the city and different places where things were going on, like the nursery district. ... We'd go there, and we'd run the kids through there, make them go to see all this stuff. You had this really rich kind of deal.

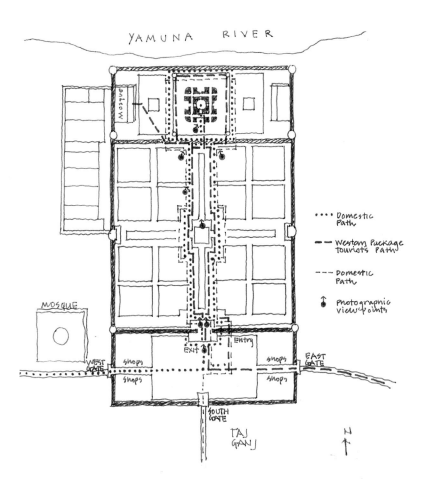

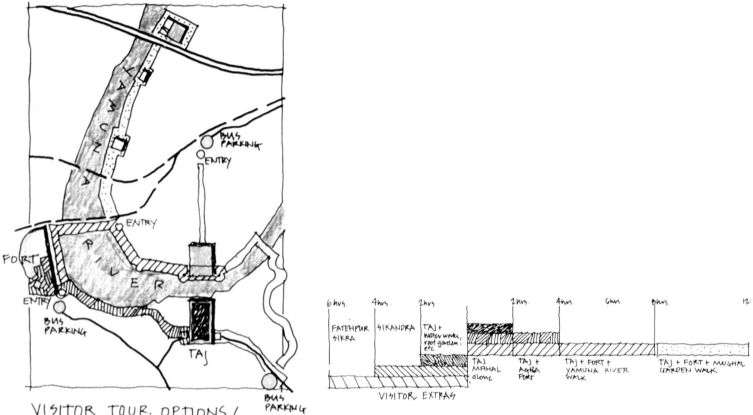

VISITOR TOUR. OPTIONS /
DURATIONS

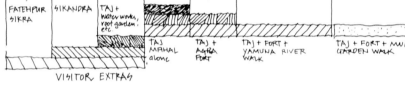

VISITOR EXTRAS

Above: Analysis of visitor duration on site

Opposite from left: Analysis of multiple overlapping view structures within the Cultural Heritage District; Daily life on the streets of the Taj Ganj neighborhood with the ghostly Taj in the distance

In the View to the Taj exercise, Terry encouraged us to see the world-famous monument as an integral part of the cultural landscape. His sketches of the Taj enabled a new way to see it, not as a stand-alone building at the edge of a walled garden, but as a backdrop to the community of people and livestock living on the flood plain, farms, and settlements on the banks of the Yamuna River. In his approach, Terry displays a similar sensibility as evident in his East Central Illinois Garden and the Foothill Mountain Observatory in California—paying careful attention to the lay of the land as shaped by intertwined natural and cultural systems. Distilling the complexity of the vernacular landscape in design proposals was his goal in Agra just as it was in his projects in the U.S. His fascination with the vernacular and his ability to interpret it through drawing is a common thread in his design projects. In Agra, too, he was drawn to the everyday life of the Yamuna riverfront. This, together with his interest in the rich history of Mughal tomb gardens, gives him a unique vantage point in assessing urban landscape heritage and advocating for its interpretation through design.

Terry's drawings have a spare, minimalist quality to them as the landscape he sees is abstracted into lines, planes, and basic forms. The views appear telescoped, offering the viewer a capacity to

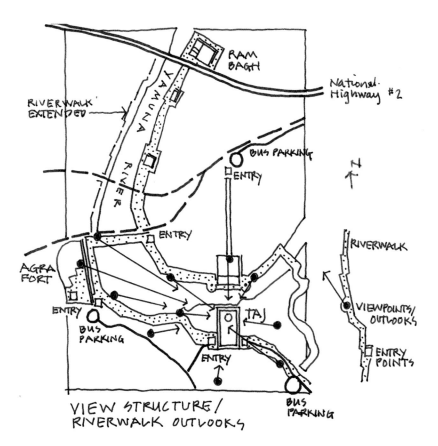

VIEW STRUCTURE /
RIVERWALK OUTLOOKS

see far but also, simultaneously, to examine things close at hand. And even though they capture views in movement, there is a stillness about the drawings. Their aesthetic stems from a detached perspective, summoning what is distant into the picture frame and bringing order and clarity along with it. The drawings are cerebral and unique—very different from the more intimate and sensual experiences in the vibrant landscapes of India that other artists attempt to portray.

Today as many cities in India invest in revitalizing their riverfronts by building promenades and ghats (stepped landings), the Taj Mahal Cultural Heritage District Development Plan remains relevant in its vision to integrate monuments with their larger surroundings and re-connect the river with the city. Terry's concepts—garden district, ensemble of heritage sites, necklace of historic buildings, River Yamuna as a frame for visitor experience of heritage—introduce a new way of seeing heritage and thinking about conservation at the urban scale in India.

¹ All site photographs and drawings, unless otherwise stated, are from the collection of the Department of Landscape Architecture, University of Illinois at Urbana-Champaign. Site photographs were taken in January 2000. The Taj Mahal project team included the faculty members Vince Bellafiore, Terrence Harkness, Ken McCown, Brian Orland, and Amita Sinha. Participating students included Melissa del Rosario, Allison Eyring, Matthew Grossman, Michael Hoffman, Johanna James, Lorne Leonard, J. Michael Loganbill, William Malone, Brandon Qualls, Andrew Stahr, Lamont Turcotte, James Urban, Peter Valicenti, and Gregory Walenter.

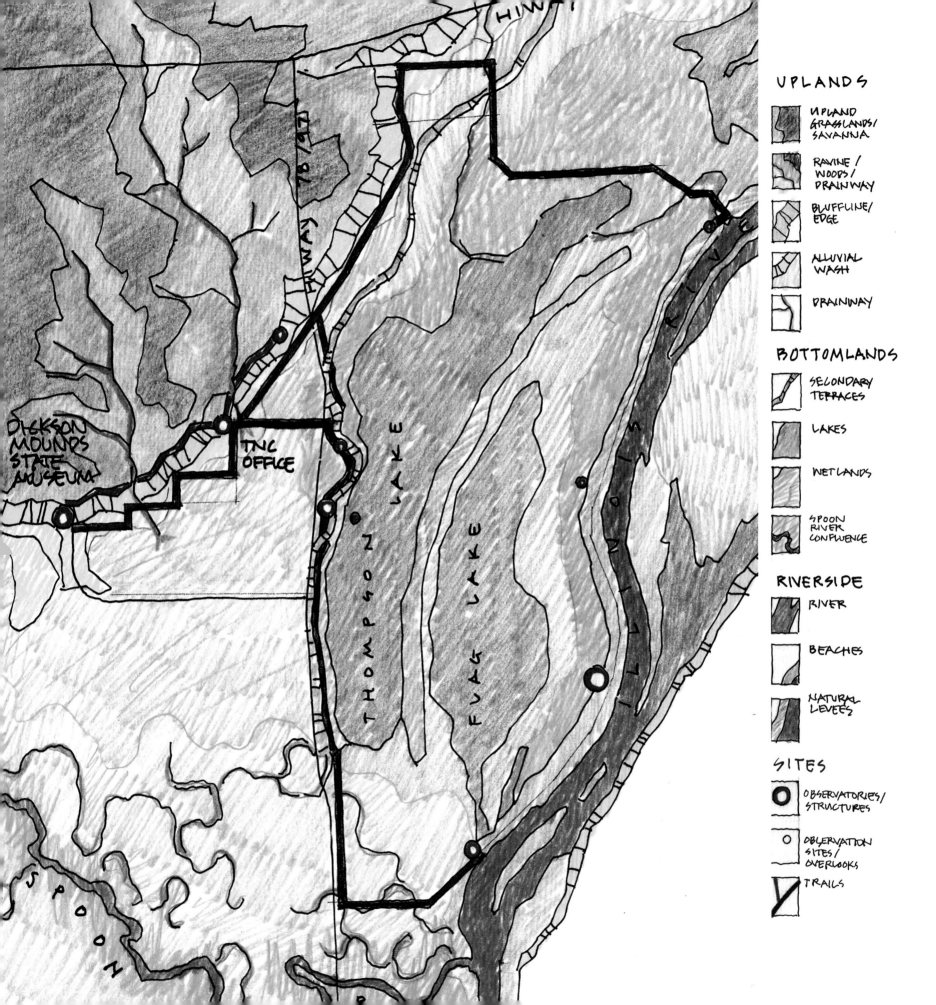

UPLANDS

UPLAND GRASSLANDS/ SAVANNA

RAVINE / WOODS/ DRAINWAY

BLUFFLINE/ EDGE

ALLUVIAL WASH

DRAINWAY

BOTTOMLANDS

SECONDARY TERRACES

LAKES

WETLANDS

SPOON RIVER CONFLUENCE

RIVERSIDE

RIVER

BEACHES

NATURAL LEVEES

SITES

OBSERVATORIES/ STRUCTURES

OBSERVATION SITES/ OVERLOOKS

TRAILS

DICKSON MOUNDS STATE MUSEUM

TNC OFFICE

HIGHWAY 78/97

THOMPSON LAKE

FLAG LAKE

ILLINOIS RIVER

SPOON

Design Without Judgment: The Emiquon Preserve

Douglas Johnston

In buying a 7000-acre farm near Havana, Illinois, The Nature Conservancy (TNC) did something unprecedented. There had been keen interest by natural resource advocates in the restoration of large floodplain river systems such as the Illinois River, which had been dammed, channeled, and drained over the past century. By acquiring an entire levee district in 2000, TNC could embark on a large-scale restoration experiment to reconnect the river to its floodplain and recreate a landscape that was already lost by the end of the 19th century. This was the genesis of the Emiquon Preserve.

TNC planned to reconstruct a stretch of the Illinois River's historic hydrologic cycle and floodplain lakes in order to increase fish and waterfowl habitat and restore historic floodplain vegetation, including wetlands, prairie, and bottomland and upland forests. However, restoration wasn't as easy as simply removing the levees that separated the bottomlands from the river. This part of the Illinois River floodplain is as flat as a pancake; small changes in water level result in very large changes in surface area. The irony was that "restoration" would require control mechanisms for very deliberate water management.

TNC's plan for restoration was challenged by other cultural factors as well. From the start, removal of productive farmland in the region challenged public understanding. To the laypersons' eyes, the crisp order of cultivated row crops would be replaced with unknown mixes of long-dormant seeds, or worse, extensive areas of mud. The Nature Conservancy would need to explain the restoration efforts in a way that could teach, interpret, and reveal the long history of human use and settlement of this landscape.

Our involvement (Terry Harkness and myself) began with an invitation from Austin Tao, a St. Louis landscape architect and Terry's former classmate, to collaborate in preparing a proposal for a visitor use plan. Recognizing that we were potentially dealing with multiple types of visitors in a very subtle and expansive site (larger than the entire Chicago Loop), the design team sought to reveal

Above: *Emiquon Preserve, Havana, IL. Before—floodplain with agricultural lands beside the levee, showing a controlled burn (photo courtesy of D. Johnston)*

Opposite: *Austin Tao Associates/ Terry Harkness/ Doug Johnston. January 2006. Emiquon Visitor Use Plan Technical Report, Historic Landscape Types (22)*

the changing landscape of the river bottomlands with a Visitor Use Plan designed around a series of landscape observatories. Following closely on the heels of Terry's work on Foothill Mountain Observatory, the Emiquon Preserve project synthesizes ideas from that project, as well as his series of Illinois gardens, into one design that is intensely of its place.

Interview with Molly Briggs and M. Elen Deming, August 1, 2011:

TGH: The Emiquon Nature Conservancy project over at Havana ... looks at the cultural components, revegetation, hydrology ... much the way it's done in the Foothill Mountain Observatory. ... It's such a wonderful place ... with the most wonderful interpretive exhibits telling about the human ecology of these landscapes. Each talks about a component of this wetland, this bottomland, and each of these are observatories that ... find the best location to tell a story about what it used to be like: the fish, vegetation, water changes, things like that. The Emiquon visitor plan tells the upland story of the [original] people, tells the bottomland story, with various kinds of vegetation, wetland, and river stories.

Above: After—floodplain with seasonal lake with distant levee and main river channel beyond (photo courtesy of Liz Vogel, May 2017)

Opposite: Austin Tao Associates/Terry Harkness/ Doug Johnston. Emiquon Visitor Use Plan Technical Report (January 2006). Design Strategies showing parking circles, bottomlands, and wetland observatory (58)

Rather than focusing on a single interpretive site, the Emiquon observatories are based on key resources distributed at key points of interest. Design principles such as contrast, overlook, panorama, and drama are key to attracting visitors. Interpretive landscape narratives are drawn from landscape conditions including water control structures, wetlands, bottomland forest, upland forests, and upland cultural features, including the nearby burial mounds and extant farm buildings. As with all of Terry's work, the landscape is the central character in the story. No real distinctions are drawn between what is "natural" and what is "cultural." The landscape integrates these seemingly opposed constructs into a coherent whole. It is the experience of the landscape that matters, and all conveniences and contrivances are directed to enhancing that.

For those traveling through the region, the experience of the Emiquon landscape occurs at 65 mph along the state highway. This limits opportunities for interpretation of the multiple-mile-long site to just two to three minutes of transit, which call for big design moves. The focus of the plan centers on the original farmstead (office, animal barns, service areas, etc.) on the premise that it was already highly disturbed, had good highway access, and enabled multiple narratives.

In situations like this, a typical response would be to build an observation tower providing a broad prospect over the entire site. We ultimately rejected this idea because we felt the landscape itself should be the draw rather than the observation structure. Landscape processes of water level change and habitat transitions should not be observed from a distance but through direct immersion.

Interview with Molly Briggs, August 8, 2011:

MCB: Lets talk about this a little bit more—about modes of viewing and relating that to moving and being still. So, by "movement arrested"— you mean viewing points. Places where you absorb the place from a fixed position.

TGH: Right. At Emiquon what we did was to figure out what were the most prominent points, the intersections with the highest potential of telling how the big system worked. Water management. Wetlands. The cultural history up on the bluff. We're looking for that place where the design, the topography, the landscape itself says "this is really important." If you have a story to tell, decide the way you lay the thing out—in this case we're talking about thousands of acres ... but even on 55 acres you have to make that decision ... and even in a Japanese garden you do that very self-consciously, in terms of how you orchestrate vision and how you bring visitors "to attention" in various ways.

Given that nearly all visitors would arrive by car, careful thought is given to the drivers' arrival experience. Because the visitor experience is intended to start from the borders of the site, not a parking lot, each observatory is provided an entry drive from the main highway. The idea of visual and physical intersection is thus a key concept in recognizing the variability of visitor capacity.

Therefore, entry roads and car parking lots are viewed as extensions of the landscape forms with loops and "parking circles" linked to the mounds and levee forms. The drives and parking circles support the casual visitor, who, even without stopping, could gain a greater understanding of the site's features. Short walks may then extend a more engaged visitor's experience up to a quarter-mile limit (similar to parking lots in relation to retail stores).

Trying to mimic historic variation in water levels poses challenges for the visitor experience. Because of its flatness, any subtle water level changes result in dramatic horizontal movement of the "shoreline" between the upland, wetland, and seasonal open water environments. Visitors understand that existing levees mediate fluctuations between the river water and bottomland water. Therefore to help visitors perceive and understand the water's changing edge, the Wetland Observatory was designed with levee-like landforms connected by boardwalks providing a fixed elevation datum. From the parking circle, visitors could follow the levee/ boardwalk to approach a wetland overlook where, at different times of year, the levee would mark changing water levels.

Having a floodplain width of several miles, the broad Illinois River valley is edged by bluffs rising 80-100 feet above the bottomlands. The upland forest and prairie that historically covered this landscape offers a distinctive contrast to the floodplain. These bluffs provided topographic connectors to bottomland camps, farmland, hunting and fishing lands, and were home to well-developed American Indian settlements. The long-term Native American history of this region is monumentalized in the construction of permanent burial mounds near the site sheltering the remains of nearly 200 people.

These mounds became a primary driver of form for our interpretive design. Mounds also offered a means of prospect formed from the landscape rather than imposed upon it—a real attraction in such a flat place. More practically, mounds also became a way of recycling acres of concrete paving around the farm operations area to form the base of the landforms. The Bluff Observatory is therefore designed to provide a panoramic oversight of the preserve, while also paying tribute to the Native American cultural history of this site.

The Bluff Observatory brings visitors to an overlook along a path that circumscribes the mounds. The observatory structures provide another unifying architectural element to the visitor experience. Building on the precedent of rural farm buildings in central Illinois, the overlook structure provides

Above: Emiquon Preserve, Havana, IL. High water conditions in floodplain lake (photo courtesy of Liz Vogel, May 2017)

Opposite clockwise from top left:
Interpretive signage and "levee" pathways as constructed at Emiquon Preserve, Havana, IL (photo courtesy of Liz Vogel, May 2017); Emiquon Preserve, Havana, IL. High water conditions in floodplain lake (photo courtesy of Liz Vogel, May 2017); Austin Tao Associates/Terry Harkness/ Doug Johnston. January 2006; Series of levee-like landforms connected by boardwalks ; Design Strategies— Wetland Observatory. Emiquon Visitor Use Plan Technical Report (59)

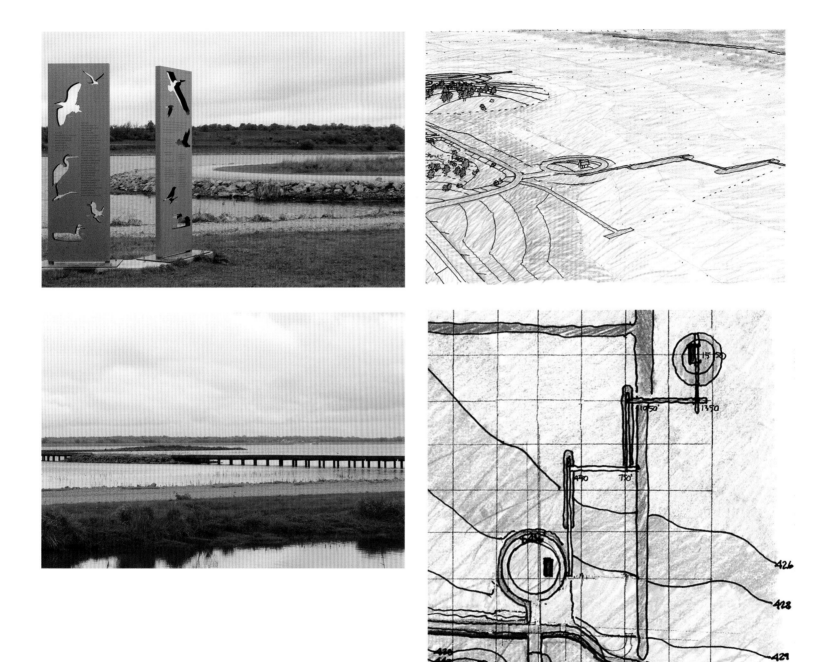

Above: View of the Illinois River Floodplain from bluff (Photos courtesy of Doug Johnston, ca. 2006)

Opposite: Emiquon Preserve, Havana, IL. Backwaters, pathways, and levees (photo courtesy of Liz Vogel, May 2017)

a familiar, yet distinctive visual element for shelter and interpretation. Simple forms sitting lightly on the landscape, these open structures were designed to provide movable barn-door walls to shelter or open up to the landscape, depending on programming or climatic opportunities. The Bluff Observatory also proposed a future trail linking the site to the nearby Dixon Mounds Museum.

Restoring river bottomlands seems to suggest the removal of agricultural drainage infrastructure and protective levees. However, the simple fact that the Illinois River is no longer a "natural river"—receiving Chicago's water discharge and dammed to support navigation—precludes any notion of ecological integrity, no matter how desirable. In fact, in the context of the urbanized watershed system of which it is a part and in order to better simulate the historic environment, the "restoration areas" are the most forcibly managed part of the overall design.

During the twentieth century, Emiquon's pump house pumped water out of the drainage district and into the Illinois River to make the land dry enough for agricultural production. Now the same pumps would be used to draw water down to mimic the annual cycle of spring flooding to summer dryness, regardless of water levels in the river channel. The levees however disconnected the historic floodplain lakes to the river channel. Because native fish species depended on the backwater lakes as part of their lifecycle, planned restoration of an open-water connection to the river was necessary. From our perspective, this provided an optimal opportunity to create a new Observatory. Exposing the infrastructure of the pump-and-river connection presented another interpretive storyline—that the preserve is an integral part of a larger interconnected and interdependent landscape system.

Ultimately the Visitor Use Plan called for design interventions on less than 3% of the Emiquon Preserve, largely on land previously disturbed from agricultural use and river channelization. The conceptual designs embedded in the plan would be used by the TNC to seek philanthropic support for the Preserve, and the implementation of the visitor support programming.

The following year, Terry Harkness and I proposed another Visitor Use Plan for Chicago Openlands' Lakeshore Preserve, the Ravine, Bluff, and Shoreline Restoration and Nature Preserve at Fort Sheridan on Lake Michigan (2006). This project benefited from rapid implementation that was relatively faithful to the proposal. However, the Emiquon Preserve Visitor Use Plan stands as a rich narrative of Terry Harkness's approach to landscape architecture at the largest scale. More than many, if not most contemporary designers, Harkness derives design forms directly from the existing landscape of the place—forms without judgment regarding the natural and cultural heritage of the place. The design is deeply, inseparably grounded to its context. The result is a familiar yet novel place.

International Software

Brenda J. Brown

I first saw the International Software campus in Fargo, North Dakota from Interstate 29, while making the 1900+ mile road trip between Gainesville, Florida and Winnipeg, Manitoba. Suddenly, to the west appeared three lush, generously large fields of reddish gold grasses, rows of Bur Oak, American Linden, Crab Apple, and Siberian Pea dividing them. It was stunning—and curiously familiar. A little further on I realized: this was Terry Harkness's work, a project in which his ideas, best known from his direct, deceptively simple, elegant drawings, have been made material.

I have since spent time in that landscape and its buildings. Here, I have thought, is a master landscape architect at the top of his game.

Interview with Molly Briggs, August 8, 2011:

> **TGH:** *Well you have to have big budgets, you know, you have real clients, you have real programs, and if what you want to do doesn't fit into the program then you don't get to do it. The reason I got to do [Great Plains / Microsoft / International Software] was because that client and that architect understood. And that's the closest I've come to it.*

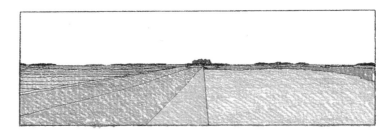

Above: *Terry Harkness, 2004. Distilling North Dakota— landscape character drawings*

Opposite: *View looking over newly established shelterbelt gardens northwest toward the "Commons" and "Vision" Building (Perkins & Will Architects), International Software campus, Fargo, ND (photo © James Steinkamp Photography, courtesy of Matt Torgerson)*

There was a time when Terry would modestly—and perhaps slyly—refer to himself as "just a regionalist landscape architect." Indeed, at the 1991 Dumbarton Oaks symposium on regionalism in American garden design one participant found it necessary to assert that there were other contemporary regionalist landscape architects besides Terry Harkness. However, while "regionalist" generally connotes someone tied to one place, Terry has delved deeply into natural and cultural landscapes of southern California and southeast North Dakota, as well as central Illinois. In 1998, in an epigraph to his description of his Foothill Mountain Observatory Terry quoted Scott Momaday: "Once in his life a man ought to concentrate his mind upon the remembered earth. ... He ought to give himself up to a particular landscape in his experience, to look at it from as many angles as he can, to wonder about it, to dwell upon it." This might be an apt introduction to any one of Terry's investigations except that he has so concentrated in several places.

Although his practice in firms, collaborative teams, and as an individual certainly includes work in cities, thus far the landscapes most prominent in his research agenda have not been urban. That research, going back to his MLA thesis, has focused on the landscape's natural base (including its expression in native plant communities) and its transformations by humans and their forms of settlement—agriculture, roads, water and soil management, farmsteads, and, sometimes, suburban dwelling. And although Terry articulated his concept of design as a "landscape observatory" beginning in 1997, he now sees it as an overarching theme in his investigations. As "landscape observatory" suggests, his abstractions of these landscape elements revolve around and intertwine with a keen sense of how they will be experienced and understood when recast in new (and smaller scale) designs. His abstractions—clean lines, crisp geometries, distilled, direct, economical—seemingly reflect a modernist sensibility, but that sensibility has almost certainly also derived, or at least been reinforced, by his self-conscious immersion in these utilitarian landscapes.

When Terry recounts his inspirations for the Fargo project he cites northeast North Dakota's extreme and variable climate, light and big sky, its expansiveness, flat horizon, shallow drainage ways and deep ditch networks, and the Euclidian geometry of its homes and farm buildings. He speaks fondly and knowledgably of the CCC shelterbelts introduced in the 1930s that now shape spacious protected outdoor rooms and inscribe tall landscape lines. He recalls how, with Matt Torgerson, he searched out, photographed, and drew distinctive natural and vernacular landscape features—from farm-field swales to flower-lined vegetable gardens—in their first summer of work together on the project more than twenty-five years ago. These landscape conditions, features, and experiences have driven the project's architecture along with its landscape design. As Terry has not infrequently and gleefully pointed out, this project has been driven by its landscape architects.

Interview with Molly Briggs and M. Elen Deming, August 1, 2011:

TGH: When I started working on [the first phase of International] Software, the founder of [Great Plains Software] ... says, "Well, you know, I think 5,000 will do it. Well! The first project will take 150,000, and probably 250,000!" So I went to a nursery and I got a plant. A little balled-and-burlapped plant. A tree—just that big. And I had someone in the parking lot. And after we made the presentation we were talking about budget. And I said, "I want you to look out the window. See that row of cars there? Can you see a tree out there?" He said, "I don't see a tree out there." I said, "Look right there. Right next to that blue car, right there." I said, "You're only going to get 250 trees like that, if you think you're getting this done for 5,000."

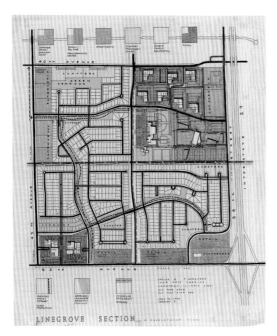 

Terry was referred to Dan Burgum, founder and owner of Great Plains Software (predecessor to International Software), by Dan Wheeler of Wheeler/Kearns in 1992. Burgum, who was from North Dakota, sought to build a campus that would further his efforts to create within his business a community culture that would reflect and strengthen the best aspects of the region. Serendipitously Matt Torgerson, a former University of Illinois graduate student from the area who had worked with Terry on other projects, was teaching in Fargo at North Dakota State University. Terry engaged him as a venture partner in a master plan intended to anticipate and accommodate future growth in the area. Matt later went to work for the original client as Leader of the Workplace Environs Team. When the site changed hands he continued there as Senior Real Estate Portfolio Manager. In essence, throughout the project, Torgerson has been a collaborator as well as the ideal client, or at least its ideal representative.

Directed to the site by Burgum, Terry and Matt found a one-mile section, a working dairy farm with a wood lot and three wind-rows of ash and poplar trees. Today, three buildings, each stylistically distinctive, all carefully set on the same ground plane, connect to one another to form a square U, arms extending west. The first and most modest "Commons" building by Wheeler/Kearns sits to the east, parallel to the interstate. The second, the "Vista" building by Julie Snow is on the north, and the third, most recent and largest "Vision" building by Perkins and Will (Ralph Johnson, principal designer) forms the southern edge of an expansive open interior landscape, much like a three-sided quadrangle or what Terry calls "the big space."

Above from left: Terry Harkness and Matt Torgerson 1998. Linegrove Section, master plan for one square mile of mixed-use development on Interstate 29, Fargo, ND; Building layers and extant shelterbelt shape an interior three-sided quadrangle, with Perkins & Will Architects (photo © James Steinkamp Photography, courtesy of Matt Torgerson)

Opposite: Terry Harkness, n.d. ca. 1993. Photograph from initial site reconnaissance and regional analysis

Interview with Molly Briggs, July 25, 2011:

TGH: Interestingly enough, this is the most successful, most cost effective, highest customer satisfaction of all [formerly] Microsoft's facilities in the world. ... So you see if this was all rural, how do you keep that kind of character when it gets all built up?

What's fun about it [pointing at the master plan] is that this is built out, this hasn't been built yet and that's not been built yet; but every time you have buildings come together you have an outdoor garden. ... That's what drives this relationship between the architecture and the landscape architecture, which is just kind of cool. What is so clear in the architect's work—and I worked with the architect really hard on it—is that this and this go together, so this connects right here, so this connects right here. So there's the outdoor kitchen and barbeque, there's a garden here, a garden here, a garden here and here, and an atrium garden here. So as you walk along, you're always looking out. You can see how it all works: how it works internally, that's how it works externally.

So anyway, what's fun about it was that really ... there is no place in this building that you can't see out. There's no place that you don't know what time of day it is, whether it's raining, sunny, if it's snowing ...

Below: *Terry Harkness, n.d. Sketch showing concept of transparency from the building lobby*

For one who knows Harkness's drawings, the shelter belt, parking lots (carefully scaled for Fargo winters) with their swales, framed fields of native grasses, and more detailed and richly planted gardens strategically located at building entrances and junctures will not be surprising. More surprising is how concerns for landscape and landscape perception have shaped the architecture. The buildings have become observatory-instruments. Intersections of outside and inside verge on seamlessness.

A CorTen steel wall spans interior and exterior of the visitors' entry atrium; the north building's walls are clad in a custom green block inside and out. Glass naturally plays a big role. Not only can one see outside from almost all the corridors, one moves along them flanked by light, the larger landscape bridged by the more intimate, complexly planted gardens that come close to invading the interior. Glass riser staircases in the two newer buildings provide nearly unobstructed access to light and views of the landscape beyond. Two large patios are physically and visually accessible to interior public spaces. One, furnished with grills, accommodates outdoor cooking as well as eating in summer. Although attention to security is evident throughout the building, an abundance of doors as well as windows bridge inside and out, and the paths through even the smaller gardens reflect the intention that they be inhabited.

Interview with Molly Briggs, July 25, 2011:

> **TGH:** *Compare that to the kind of detail you have here, I mean this is arboretum degree of complexity. In other words, there's five levels of planting there. There's [extant] trees, there's [formal] trees, there's shrubs, there's low shrubs, there's ground cover, there's perennials, there's ephemeral—all that stuff is happening right in here. You don't usually get that. The [original] client knew but [later clients] didn't know; we did it anyway, because it was important.*

Above from left: Transparency. From inside the Vision Building looking north to Vista Building across quadrangle (photo courtesy of Brenda Brown); Interstitial courtyards (photo © James Steinkamp Photography, courtesy of Matt Torgerson)

Within the references to and framing of the expansive high plains landscape, there is also great attention to detail. The often intricately layered landscapes of the gardens, some of whose richness, Terry asserts, approaches that of an arboretum, nestle within the broad strokes. (Recently, in response to employees' keen interest, Terry now plans to label all the campus's plants.) The most abstract garden fits into the L southwest of Julie North's "Vista" building; its rows of benches and line of rocks (now complimented by the carefully composed rock pile anchoring one of the south building entrances) suggest lines of glacier advance and retreat. Red maples define its north edge and also accentuate and ground the building.

Just to the south another "garden"—a double-rowed remnant of a north-south ash-poplar shelterbelt/swale with volunteer farm grasses—offsets any sense of preciousness that the manicured, distilled area might suggest. Landscape remnants continue to the north where a similar east-west shelterbelt partly shields the building's long entry and provides a transition between a parking lot and the miniature viewing gardens bordering the building. The most captivating remnant is a woodlot whose old trees—mostly ash with some Bur Oak and American Linden—have been

enhanced by plantings of ferns, hostas, red-twigged dogwood, and viburnum. One experiences it through glass on two levels of the north building and via a curved, covered causeway connecting north and east buildings, an evolution from an earlier design's open-air elevated path. It is enchanting to traverse the passage, but its structure also acts as a foil to the orthogonal geometries otherwise pervasive throughout the site.

The research agenda Terry has articulated and is best known for may obscure his concern and skill in understanding what people need. And responding to how people use and inhabit the places he designs has never been at odds with his larger research agenda. Even as a student I was impressed with his shrewd evaluations, how he seemingly effortlessly integrated principles and understandings then new to me from courses on behavioral and social considerations in design. At Fargo, Matt conducted surveys and interviews on employee satisfaction and their preferences became part of the design criteria. These, along with power optimization concerns, helped shape continuing developments of both architecture and landscape. The resulting specifications guided interior acoustics requirements (it is a markedly quiet building even when most alive with people) as well as low light levels and the size and accessibility of parking lots.

Interview with Molly Briggs, August 8, 2011:

MCB: What do you think it is about this particular client—what is it about their thinking that made them want this kind of project?

TGH: Because the founder grew up in rural ND, in Arthur, ND, and his family had farms. His uncle had grain

elevators, probably 25 of them, and he built his corporate culture on the values and ethics of an agrarian life. Service, dependability, follow-through; a whole bunch of things that were built into differentiating this software company that built medium-sized businesses. The software that his company came up with was meant for grain elevators in the rural upper provinces. ... And so, to differentiate himself from other competitors, they built it on service, not on exotic features and unfinished software and no relationship to the company that designed it. Their whole ethic was to develop a relationship between the people who sold software and the customers who bought their product. ... They had a culture, a relationship that he felt was North Dakotan and rural and kind of wild. Fargo is a growing metropolitan area. It has the youngest metro population of any city around ... The employees were local people who worked with the local universities.

They took great pride. The work ethic—all this stuff was reinforced. They had been in 50 different sites in Fargo ... he wanted to get his employees together in one building. There's an award—he used to compete [for] and for ten years running they either won it or came in second for their business category, whatever it was. When they built a new building, they wanted to have the building and the site express all of that.

In the 25-plus years that the Fargo project encompasses, housing development has expanded south some two miles to reach the International Software campus. Although Terry and Matt intensely explored the contemporary landscape they found initially, that landscape is gradually disappearing, at least closest to Fargo. And so, curiously, though not originally intended, the Fargo project may also come to be about a past landscape, a landscape constructed for collective memory as well as a contemporary place of inhabitation.

Reflections

International Software campus, Fargo, ND. Panorama from Interstate 29 looking west (photo © James Steinkamp Photography, courtesy of Matt Torgerson)

Place-Based Pedagogy

M. Elen Deming

Interview with Molly Briggs and M. Elen Deming, August 1, 2011:

> **TGH:** *This is what Vince [Bellafiore] always said. He said, "All you do is tell teaching stories, Terry."*
> *And he's right. Everything I do is about teaching somebody something.*

Paralleling the design projects showcased in this book, Harkness's long teaching career stands, for many, as his greatest achievement. His approach to professional instruction integrates conceptual, formal, and technical processes on multiple levels. Course syllabi integrate technical subjects such as plant materials, construction, irrigation, and grading, with vivid investigations of region and place. In particular, students remember Harkness for the immersive choreography of his field trips where they become sensitized to seeing the relationships between cultural and organic form. Arguably, the culmination of Harkness's intellectual discoveries are best represented in his teaching for, even as we delight in the clarity of his drawings or formal juxtaposition of textures, his design also teaches.

Interview with Molly Briggs, August 8, 2011:

> **TGH:** *This actually explains why I've been [teaching] for thirty years. … it's always "Why"? Why is something the way it is? I'm never satisfied. What's going on here? When I go places I spend time; I walk through towns trying to figure out what's going on. How do people make a living? How does this work? That's what this is all about.*
>
> **MCB:** *And it's immediately viable on two major levels. One is about understanding the world around you better; the other is just developing the capacity to pay attention. Right? All the time, anywhere. The whole world is strange.*
>
> **TGH:** *Right. Pay attention. Come to attention. I would tell the students, okay, are we coming to attention here?*

Harkness's gifts as an educator have been well recognized, including the 1990 Award for Outstanding Educator from the Council of Educators in Landscape Architecture and his elevation as a Fellow in 1994 by the American Society of Landscape Architects. But on the eve of his retirement, Harkness received the capstone of his teaching career with ASLA's Jot D. Carpenter Teaching Medal (2007). The Carpenter Medal is the field's most prestigious award for sustained and significant contributions to education in landscape architecture.

Supporting letters for his nomination were written by a host of colleagues and leaders in the field including Gary Hilderbrand, Joan Iverson Nassauer, Mark Strieter, Michael Van Valkenburgh, and

James Wescoat. Their letters stand as enduring tributes to the quality and impact of his teaching. Then Head of the Department of Landscape Architecture, James Wescoat introduced the nomination:

> Like Jot Carpenter at OSU, and Stan White and Chuck Harris before him here at Illinois, Terry Harkness's greatest intellectual passion is teaching landscape architectural design. Like Carpenter, he can hardly contain himself physically or intellectually when exploring design ideas, especially planting design, in the studio. He moves seamlessly from the lucid presentation of a complex design issue to the class as a whole, to respectful questioning in a jury, to the active listening in one-on-one desk critiques that bring out the best in young designers.

Wescoat enumerated several key components of Harkness's teaching approach, including his exhaustive development of unique "one-off" studio project sets; staging multiple simultaneous studio options to inculcate both collaboration and independence among students; the art of mastering technical craft in design; and of course his emphasis on deep understanding of locale. Among several other eminent colleagues, Joan Nassauer (University of Michigan) wrote, "Terry's work has been driven by his easy fluidity as a designer and his lively intellectual curiosity. Equally important, his career has been guided by deep personal integrity—in his relationships with people and in his management of intellectual endeavors. Students and colleagues have benefited enormously from his propensity to *include and work collaboratively* in new endeavors."

Michael Van Valkenburgh wrote, "Terry Harkness is one of a long stream of great teachers at the University of Illinois … Terry exemplifies what Jot [Carpenter] would have admired in an educator— the optimism, the love of students, the dedication, the ability to love seeing young men and women succeed." In his letter of support, Gary Hilderbrand writes that Harkness is "a giant among teachers of our field—one of the truly great figures in landscape architecture education," whose teaching emanates from "the relationship between his own investigative design work and his pursuit of knowledge."

Retiring in 2007 as Professor *emeritus* of landscape architecture, Harkness is still a sought-after design critic and guest lecturer who holds students in thrall. It is exceptionally rare to find faculty who can rise to the challenge of teaching with the same level of passionate and also intimate landscape literacy as Terry Harkness. Whether entering academic or professional pursuits, students need more teachers like Harkness to provide them with solid grounding in a place-based pedagogy.

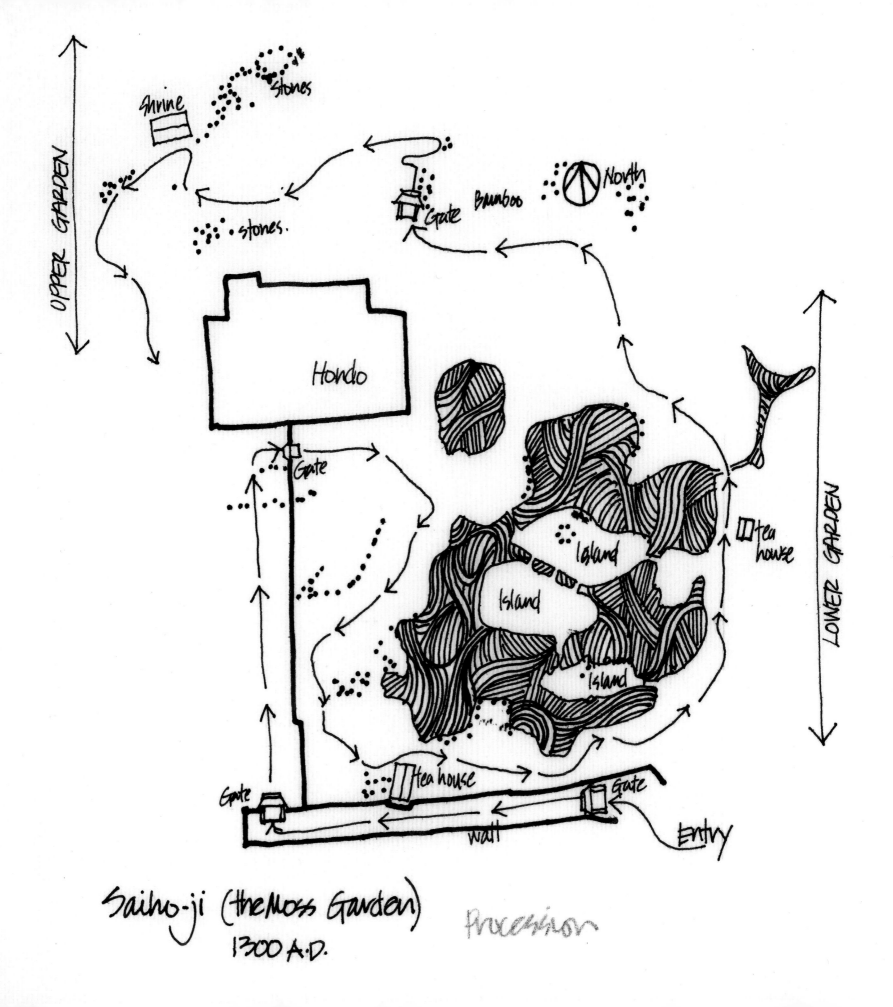

UPPER GARDEN

Shrine

stones

stones.

Gate Bamboo

North

LOWER GARDEN

Hondo

Gate

Island

Island

Island

tea house

Gate

tea house

Gate

wall

Entry

Saiho-ji (the Moss Garden)
1300 A.D.

Procession

A Design Educator

Brenda J. Brown

Interview with Molly Briggs and M. Elen Deming, August 1, 2011:

> *TGH: The first semester I taught, I was assigned to teach the history of landscape architecture! What are you doing? You've never taught before, so why don't you teach History of Landscape Architecture?!*

When I think of Terry Harkness during my student years at the University of Illinois I think first of the slightly impish character that presided in his office on Nevada Street. He sits on one side of a large wooden table facing out a large window to the north, trace paper and color markers near at hand. Nearby too is the stuff of Terry's ongoing investigations—pop-up books, postcards, and design books, his own photographs, analyses, drawings and plans as well as students' work. There is also a sort of doll bearing an uncanny resemblance to the man (I always imagined it had been a gift from someone in his family). Over time, I naturally developed a more informed and nuanced picture of him as a thoughtful, diplomatic, and often clever strategist, determinedly positive, yet at the same time not one to suffer fools gladly. Although to my knowledge he always kept his commitments, and generously gave his time to students, somewhat paradoxically he would never be found when he did not want to be.

Of course he was, as he continues to be, a committed designer and educator with strong convictions in both arenas. Terry frequently observes that his role as a professor and a practitioner are not so different; both are about educating. Matt Torgerson, who worked with Terry in both roles, finds it difficult to distinguish between the two. Nevertheless, Matt notes Terry's attentive responsiveness, adaptability, and respect in dealing with clients and points out: "He can make things seem so simple, so distilled, that people do not realize how deeply and carefully he has considered them."

Above: *Sophomore studio design jury with Terry Harkness, Robert Riley, D. Fairchild Ruggles and David Hays (photo courtesy of Misa Inoue, Spring 2011)*

Opposite: *Harkness, n.d. ca. 1970-73. sketch explaining processional route at Saihoji Moss Garden, Kyoto, Japan; course lecture from History of World Landscapes*

Interview with Molly Briggs and M. Elen Deming, August 1, 2011:

> *MCB: I've heard you say, both in print and in person, that all of your work is both didactic and experiential. How do those things happen together and how do you deal with the fact that people have to pay attention on different levels at the same time in order to get it?*
>
> *TGH: Here's what I learned from Stan White. Stan White would go out on these trips, wonderful, experiential. He'd blindfold people in the studio, and he'd give them things. He'd give them a lemon (remember when lemon juice used*

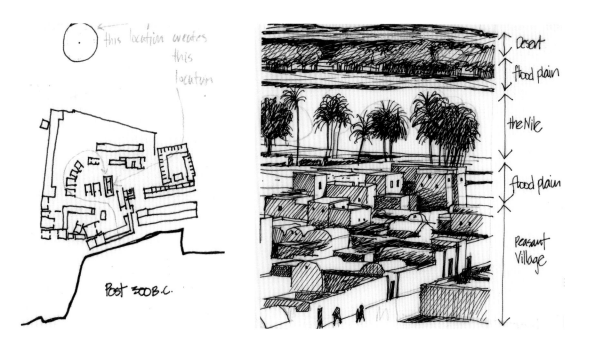

to be in a little thing, a little can?) and he'd do stuff like that. And he'd give them sensory, experiential quizzes, inside and outside the classroom.

The point being ... for instance, whether you're studying individual plants or communities, you need to go to these places that epitomize what it is. Because when you're trying to understand the plants as they make up a community you're trying to bring kids to the experience of seeing it, writing about it, sketching it, photographing it; so I would give them a whole bunch of exercises. One [exercise] is they have to follow five plants throughout the year ... I tend to be pretty verbal and do a lot of outrageous stuff when we're out looking at plants. Talking about what it is, what it looks like, time of year, of day, soil moisture, microclimate, sun aspect—to get them to follow plants throughout the year. They have to photograph, draw, describe. Color chips. You see color embedded in a woods or a ground layer or like this, you think about color and light. Is the light behind the plant? Coming this way? Doing both? Is it foggy?

We look at a ravine and a bottomland and a hill prairie and a savannah. Trying to get the kids to be away. We use photos not to be lazy but to capture experiential or atmospheric or light conditions. You've got to understand what you can do with things. Is sunlight coming through the plants? By photography they realize the difference from drawing, which is more structural. ... I learned from Stan White that teachers don't get excited often enough about what they're doing. So I used to get excited. The point is, there's some essential things you're trying to get at.

What you're trying to do is get the kids to be aware. ... Get them to capture the essential—because it all comes back to this, the essential characteristics of landscape experience.

While Terry might seem absorbed in his own work to the point of obsession, in reviews he quickly grasped what each student aimed for and just as quickly pointed out how they could achieve it.

In these, as in other situations, he displayed an ability to tune in to a wide array of students and somehow deal with each one on her or his terms.

It can be difficult for former students to discern what they have actually learned from a teacher and what that maestro somehow nurtured and/or encouraged. Terry used to differentiate two kinds of teachers: one who passes along his or her own aesthetic and methods; the other more concerned with helping students find their own way. I have come to see these designations as two extremes, two poles of a continuum, partly because what I have learned from Terry spans the categories.

Interview with Molly Briggs, August 8, 2011:

TGH: I'd try crazy stuff with the kids just because I liked to do it and I wanted to have a certain level of outrageousness. Stan White was that way. Stan White would come up to your table, and you'd be doing a wash rendering. And he says, "If you want to you can use coffee, in layers. If you want." And then he'd spill coffee on your rendering! And then he'd make it work. Some students just were livid. And some students loved it! You talk to alums, and they either hated it or they loved it. I would never do that, but ...

You really want [students] to be more self conscious about the experiences they're having, but then you have to give them a whole menu of experiences to think about. ... Because otherwise you don't get to the heart of the program and if you don't teach it the way you're thinking about it or the way ... I remember Stan White doing it, and I only had studied with him for one semester, but I remember he was so eccentric. He let you feel what he felt, or sometimes he'd create a situation or make you do strange things.

I used to have students lie down and get underneath a burning bush in the fall with the sunlight on it. There's some really big ones over at the corner of Nevada and Goodwin ... You get underneath it when the sun's on the top of that thing it and whoa! Doctor! That's what you're trying to get at.

Other former students I have talked with generally agree about Terry's qualities, style, and character, although each will cite different lingering influences. For Matt, becoming a student in the MLA program at Illinois opened up an ongoing chapter of dynamic interchange and work with Terry. Misa Inoue, with her interest in abstract transdisciplinary principles, quotes Terry: "Once you get the abstract straight, the rest of the design comes more easily," and gratefully remembers how Terry left her alone to figure out her knotty design problems. Another former student, Mark Strieter (Nelson Byrd Woltz), calls Terry "a pivotal educator" who "inspires, engages, and draws students to an institution," and whose design process of rooting a design in the cultural and native landscape is the "foundation for my design process today."

"I am beginning to understand how you work," I seem to remember Terry saying to me. I recall times when Terry succinctly sized up some aspect of my endeavors and offered observations that

to reveal complexity and subtlety of resource [resultant]

LANDSCAPE OBSERVATORY: a case study

NORTH AMERICAN [late] PLEISTOCENE LANDSCAPE ORIGINS/PROCESSES.

climate shifts   tectonic plates   ocean currents.

- GLACIAL PROCESS / CLIMATE CHANGE

- FLUVIAL / MELTWATER PROCESS.

- AEOLIAN PROCESS

- VEGETATION MIGRATION / REFUGIA.
    - tundra · arctic   cold   Dry.
         alpine
    - taiga/Boreal cold   Wet.
      forest /Muskeg.
    - Deciduous   cold   Wet.
      Forest.
    - Grassland   warm   Dry.
- FIRE ECOLOGY / REGIMES

  p r o c e s s   d e s c r i p t o r s

CULTURAL HISTORY SITES
CONSTRUCTED / RESTORED. SITES.
Interpretative OBSERVATORIES.

- LOWLAND / RIVER SITES.
    - Havana.
    - Kampsville Site/
      Center for Amer. Archeo.
    - Elared House/
    - St. Gen.   /Mo.
      American Bottoms
      Run Sites.
    - Cahokia Mounds St.
      Park.
    - Dickson Mounds St. Park.

- BLUFF / RIDGE SITES
    - Galena / IL.

CONSTRUCTED. /
INTERPRETATIVE.
OBSERVATORY

BURGUM   redriver
RIVER   oxbow
BENDS   Site
FARM   oak/linden
          woods...
          prairie
          border.
          savanna.

SITE A   Dahlen Esker/
          Glacial Meltwater.

SITE B   Gleason Sand
          Prairie / Havana
          Outwash.

SITE C   Revis Hill Prairie/
          River bluff/Aeolian
          Glacial Deposit

SITE D   Heron Pond/
          Lowland Swamp.

SITE E   Bealls Woods/
          Lowland

SITE F   Duffin Woods
          Upland Forest.

SITE G   Sibley Woods/
          Prairie Grove.

SITE H   Weston/Lodi
          Prairie/ tallgrass
          prairie

NATURE   Existing
PRESERVES Exemplars.

- written narrative
  and diagrams
  [25 pp.]
- exemplar sites
  documented
- composite
  natural sites
  observatory
- case study site/
  observatory

5

still provide self-navigating touchstones. I am uncertain if my interest in landscape interpretation, engagement, and revelation came from Terry, but certainly he encouraged it. When Terry would talk to me about the importance of conveying to others how wonderful our designs are I always felt that he was speaking from his own experience. Perhaps more definitely, from him began my care in documenting projects, my fascination with plant's potential in design, and my understanding and practice of design as research, for, whatever his other methods, Terry also teaches by example.

Interview with Molly Briggs, August 8, 2011:

On Teaching Site Design

MCB: What about working with students and getting them to develop something that makes sense from the ground when they start out in plan? How do you get them from plan view to an on-the-ground kind of understanding?

TGH: Well. I had strategies. I had some students who never understood space; they just never understood physical dimensions. So I used 3 x 5 cards and said, "On a minimum of 20 to 50 cards, I want you to write down the experience you want someone to have as they go through your garden. What are all the experiences you want them to have?" And they go, "Well, what do you mean by that?"

MCB: So that's before they're doing any formal work, right?

TGH: Yes. That's just one approach ... it gets back to landscape memory, stories, and learning, and then making places.

Here is another way, the process way. You know, if you have a park or a school or a residence, you already know a whole bunch about it programmatically. There's an entry, a bedroom, a classroom, a dining room, whatever. You know all these things. So [I ask the students to] zone that out. Tell me what it is. Tell me what those relationships are. What are the critical relationships? That's the functional diagram.

Another thing I used to tell students—because you never know which door you're going to get them through, they all go through a different door—another door I used to show them is, okay, what are the landscape concepts? Is it a parkland, or a mountain, is it a valley? Is it a thicket? A spring woodland that you remember? Or a high mountain lake? Is there something here that you could, in a similar way, begin to sketch for me? I want one of these, one of these, one of these. Okay, now: how do you put those together? Is there an organizational order? How do you move through it? How do you circulate? There's a bunch of different ways to do that.

Once you have this, then you say, "Well, how do I want the story to unfold? Where do we start, where do we end, where do we have our big wonderful thing? Where is the building or the garden going to be?" ... Then we know, for instance, what is the spatial structure of this functional stuff? Is it a big space or a long hallway? It can be large or medium or small. Your project may have all of these, or parts of them, or the illusion of parts of them.

This [illusion] is what's so interesting about Japanese or Chinese gardens. I saw a garden at Daitoku-ji called the Daisen-in; the garden is no bigger than this room, but it's really about the world, the Shinto world or the Japanese world of ocean, mountain, island—in this little tiny space. It's all there! [It] had the traditional elements—rock being

Opposite: *Terence Harkness n.d. Landscape Observatory: A Case Study; handwritten course syllabus for Natural Precedent in Planting using regional sites*

mountain, raked sand being ocean, plants being forests, and so on. You can invoke any kind of scale you want, that's not the problem. Students think it is, but it's not.

So ... [students] could ... look at any one of these gardens and say, oh! I get how that works... Then you start thinking, what do I want this to be? What is the structure of the thing, what are its functional relationships—and then what do I want to make out of it? All of this is trial and error—try it on, change it, and it just goes back and forth. Then you make all kinds of detail decisions; every one of these goes back and forth. Is this the right side? Is the building elevated, is it lower? .... you're going back and forth, back and forth, all the time.

Interviews with Molly Briggs and M. Elen Deming, August 1, 2011:

Teaching through Field Trips

I would orchestrate field trips like a play. ... I had two or three big day trips. I'd start over at The Vermilion River, then to [Russell] Duffin Woods [Nature Preserve], where the oak/hickory forest meets beech/maple, over at Forest Glen. The big deal would be the last site. The last site should always be the most exciting, late in the afternoon the lighting is very different from where we started out at 1:00.

They have these wonderful ravines with dogwoods, where they're really protected under this real high canopy. Then you'd go to an oak/hickory woods and check the humidity—very different. The light is different. Oak/hickories are a much droughtier, drier place, so if I went all the way down to southern Illinois you'd really feel the change in humidity. We might start at Vermilion and then go to Lake of the Woods. There's a really nice bottomlands woods there. ... A lowland woods has a very different feel than a ravine woods. The stuff you're going to get in a bottomland can survive flooding—there's a whole set of trees and shrubs that can do that.

Dogwoods want to be sheltered, they don't want to be at the edge of the woods, so instead you see redbuds at the edge. If you go at the right time in spring you'll see exactly what the diagram is for redbuds and dogwoods. Redbuds are always at the edge. Dogwoods are inside. Dogwoods are in shelter, higher humidity. Same thing with a prairie crab-apple—they're the first to bloom. Yet you see they're always in disturbed situations. They can take a lot of heat, they can take dry, and they're always along edges of woods. They're before redbuds; dogwoods are after redbuds. So all of a sudden you see all this situational fit.

You go across and introduce [students] to prairies, to wet and mesic and dry prairies, and we end up on the Illinois River, by Havana. We'll see these hill prairies up on top of the bluffs. It's so dry on these hill prairies ... above the limestone bluffs, the plants you see are prairie plants that should be out in Kansas and Nebraska, with 10 to 15 inches of rain, versus the 40 that we get. Not only the grasses, but there are all these other critters that would only be found in these conditions. When there is wildfire or when the farmer would burn off the edge of the fields, the fire might get up on these hill prairies and burn it off. But if you take the fire away, it's all junipers and red cedar. So now you see all the hill prairies disappearing and up on the hilltops you see all these red cedars.

The whole point on the experiential thing is, whatever you're doing, it's particular in terms of this: I want [students] to learn plant types, and I have several strategies [for that]. We show it to them, they get it out of books, we show them in plan... I want them to understand that in 15 years the scale changes. ...I've got a whole set of exercises [about this]. If you have gone to see it and drawn it and you've photographed it, then you can say, okay, these are all the plants that fit into that type... You try to get them to think like this. Then we pull it together and say, okay this is a beech maple forest; this is an oak hickory forest; and we have these things sorted out so they can have some conceptual framework.

Prairie Plantsman

James Wescoat

Of Terry Harkness's deeply insightful and creative qualities, his passion for plants and planting deserves special recognition. In the early 2000s, Terry picked me up at the airport for my first visit to the University. A light rain made the plant leaves glossy and rich in hue, richness I would later recognize in his color pencil drawings. Coming from semi-arid Colorado I was amazed to see plants I had studied far south in Louisiana but had not seen when living a bit further north in Chicago. Terry affirmed, yes, indeed we do have bald cypress trees here in east central Illinois, lots of them, and sweet gum, Ginkgo biloba, of course, and more. He enjoyed introducing us to grand and less familiar species, on this occasion culminating in the truly magnificent oaks across the parking lot from Temple Hoyne Buell Hall. I imagine first encounters with Terry Harkness may often revolve around the beauty and character of trees.

Terry is also generous with his knowledge of native perennials that, in the profession of landscape architecture, tend to receive somewhat less attention than woody plants. Urbana-Champaign has a passionate community of prairie grass and wildflower enthusiasts so he is in good company. He introduced us to the work of SIU botanist Robert Mohlenbrock and UIUC's prairie botanists like Ken Robertson, John Taft, and others.

On the University of Illinois campus, Terry has mixed his labor admirably with his planting design sensibilities. On one occasion he tackled the steep slope on the northwest corner of the Temple Hoyne Buell grass amphitheatre. He included favorites like Prairie dropseed that had special promise. Unstable soil, full exposure, no irrigation, Terry with a straw hat, and a team of students planting on the slope—and then alone watering by hand weeks later until they were established.

In nominating Terry for the Jot Carpenter Medal in 2007, I wrote about the way he taught his regional planting design studios, "starting with natural vegetation transects across the length and breadth of the vegetation assemblages in Illinois, so that students develop an understanding of vegetation while they begin to think about planting. He does this in ways that complement the botanist's ideas about vegetation, e.g., by having students select an individual plant in a natural ecosystem and revisit it in every season of the year, documenting its changing relationships with surrounding plants."

In the halls and in studio, we lamented concepts like "plant materials," as if living beings could be compared with varieties of concrete. Discussion of planting aesthetics could drift into plant history and ethics—but even more so and far more often into his exclamations of pure wonder and delight, "Oh! Whoa! Now that is it, that is truly it!"

Above: *Terry Harkness and his straw hat; prairie slope restoration (photo courtesy of Elen Deming, September 2012)*

Opposite: *Prairie Slope restoration and oaks at Temple Buell Hall, University of Illinois (photo courtesy of Liz Vogel, June 2017)*

Borrowed Landscapes:
Transforming the University

M. Elen Deming with Kathleen Harleman

Despite his official retirement from academic life in 2007, Terry Harkness remains ever-present at the University of Illinois. In addition to his active design consultancy on projects from Florida to California, he maintains a heroic planting design and maintenance portfolio that continues to transform the Urbana campus. Harkness recently designed the Sesquicentennial Garden for the grounds of the University President's House, advises on planting installations at the University of Illinois Arboretum, and continues to steward several gardens in the heart of campus near the intersection of the South Quad and the Military Axis.

The University's collection of extant "Harkness" gardens include the prairie slope restoration at Temple Buell Hall and the H.I. and Mabery D. Gelvin Garden at the Krannert Art Museum (KAM). Terry also maintains gardens designed by others, including two by former students. Dave Frigo (Hitchcock Associates) designed the roof garden planters at the College of Education and Gina Gianetti designed the Darlene Schantz Memorial Garden north of the Link Gallery, for the School of Art & Design. Notably, since 2010, Terry Harkness and Master Gardener Gloria Rainer have guided and worked side by side with a dedicated corps of volunteers maintaining KAM's Gelvin Garden in peak condition year round. Terry's rule of thumb for health and happiness? "Spend a minimum of two hours at work in the garden every day—rain or shine."

Interview with Molly Briggs and M. Elen Deming, August 1, 2011:

MCB: What about the work you're doing with the Krannert Art Museum? And do you work a garden at your own home?

TGH: I've got about five gardens I take care of. I just travel around. I have to be outside. I finally realized if I'm not out half the day I'm not a happy person.

Landscape tends, almost by definition, to be a conservative medium. Landscape design conventions are often far slower to give way to new values and ideas than, say, architecture or the visual arts. It is thus not surprising that, during the course of his career at the University of Illinois, Terry's vision

Above from top: *Roof garden with with prairie perennials at the College of Education, University of Illinois (photo courtesy of Liz Vogel, June 2017); Members of the Gelvin Garden Committee, Krannert Art Museum (photo courtesy of Julia Kelly, July 2015)*

Opposite: *Prairie Slope restoration at Temple Buell Hall, University of Illinois (photo courtesy of Liz Vogel, June 2017)*

for campus has sometimes exceeded his ability to advocate for—not to mention the University's readiness to accept—a different kind of landscape sensibility. As in many of his earlier projects, Terry Harkness "borrows" the subtle forms and logic of the regional landscape in designs for smaller spaces on campus. These campus gardens, in turn, awaken students to ephemeral processes and seasons taking place in larger landscapes, beyond the bounds of their sight and senses, in order to tell them where in the world they really are.

GROVE / SWALE / FIELD INTERSECTION   Krannert swale garden

Unrequited Design. Two notable examples where Terry's design intentions have remained unrealized are the Gelvin Garden at Krannert Art Museum (KAM) and the regional airport (University of Illinois Willard Airport).

The H.I. Gelvin and Mabery D. Gelvin Garden. As originally designed in 1961, the Krannert Art Museum featured a shallow white marble reflecting pool that linked the site with the building's elegant facade. After maintenance of the pool was determined to be too resource intensive, the College of Fine & Applied Arts asked Terry Harkness to produce design alternatives, including one for a traditional perennial border and bowling green. Eventually, the basin was filled with soil, vegetated with turf grass and, in 1990, Rosann Gelvin Noel, a generous philanthropist, dedicated The H.I. Gelvin and Mabery D. Gelvin Garden to the memory of her parents.

En route to that decision, however, Terry had explored an alternative scheme with component forms characteristically evocative of the regional Illinois landscape. Where the modernist reflecting pool had once fetishized water as a pristine mirror of architectural perfection, Terry envisioned the garden as an exhibition in itself—displaying the hydrological phases, associated plant communities, and drainage structures devised by Illinoisans to ensure peaceful coexistence with a mutable landscape. Sadly, he was unable to persuade the University to build this rather less conventional design proposal—one he still considers among his best work. Years later, although the Gelvin Garden as built is much beloved, Terry still feels the missed opportunity keenly. "This is the art for what wasn't built at Krannert Art Museum," he laments. "Now that is a story that I can barely tell. It's very painful."

Willard Regional Airport. Another unrequited proposal is Terry's design for the University of Illinois's Willard Airport—the regional airport serving greater Champaign County. As in all his work, Terry believes landscape design has the capacity to tell teaching stories about the origins and formation of cultural landscapes. And nowhere does a designed landscape have greater capacity and responsibility to tell people where they are than at the regional airport, seen as it is from both aerial and ground perspectives at different scales and speeds of perception. In a white paper he presented to University officials, Terry describes the design opportunities presented by the regional airport.

> "Landscape Design: The Common Landscape, Presence and Response, Continuity and Change"
>
> An airport is an everyday kind of experience for most of us. The idea behind this proposal is to allow the traveler, as well as the resident, to read the landscape by juxtaposition and by comparison. The larger landscape of East Central Illinois is subtle: it is boring to some and endlessly variable to others. The design concept of the airport site is similar to the idea of a demonstration garden—the distillation and demonstration of several essential experiences and patterns of the larger landscape. The issue is, can we reveal this place for those who arrive and depart? What overall process, specific environmental issues or histories are memorable in this landscape?
>
> The landscape is the Jeffersonian square mile grid that starts in Ohio and works its way west. For many years the landscape was simply a swampy wetland one could only paddle a canoe across in the spring. Only when the German settlers came and the drainage control legislation was passed could these settlers tile, drain, and channel the land so they could farm. … The airport and its runways nest in the matrix of the larger farmed landscape that is inscribed by the square mile grid. These two existing patterns reveal the design approach of bringing our abstracted elements of the landscape into vivid intersection and juxtaposition. …

We can begin to develop the heightened experience of the Illinois landscape at ground level by bringing the major vegetative communities of East Central Illinois together on the terminal site. From out of the window of the aircraft, on the ground with your car, when coming home in summer or in fall the planted scene will continually change and reveal the crops, the grasses, the trees, the plowing, the snow and drifting patterns. ... As you arrive and depart through this regional airport, you are in a prairie, you are in a grassland, you are in a burr oak grove community, you are in a farm cropland community.

[Another] aspect of design organization is how human history reveals its aspects and forms of the region. There are several precedents from the local scene that are powerful reminders of how man has come to terms with this landscape ... the early paving of the state-supported road system and the rural drainage districts and their common drainage ditches. ... Civic Improvement Associations promoted tree plantings along these rights of way. Some of those trees can still be seen today.

Whether [arriving or departing] by plane or by car, one is confronted with these visible cultural and environmental benchmarks or gauging stations. This is what is meant at the very beginning ... about our ability as designers to tell the storys [sic] of the landscape, of culture in an abstracted, distilled way. To involve others in the creation of manmade places is a heightened way of sensing the past, the present, and perhaps a future.

Below from left: Terry Harkness, n.d. Regional Airport Synthesis. Plan diagrams showing strategies for drainage, formal definition of edges, and planting design; Terry Harkness, n.d. Airport Arrival Sequence. Sketch study showing strategies for roadway alignment, water management, and plant communities

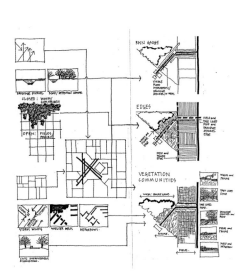

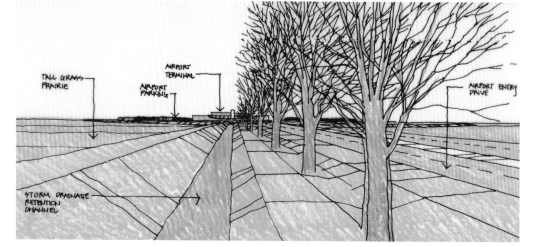

In a series of analyses consistent with his HOK process, Terry studied patterns of climate (wind direction and control), hydrology, topography (young glacial till plain), vegetation (open and closed forms), and ownership patterns (square mile grid). He produced a sectional analysis showing how roadway and railroad embankments lift travelers above wet surfaces. Similar to Foothill Mountain

Observatory, the airport arrival sequence functions as an observatory with "instrumentation" designed to reveal characteristic forms, processes, and cultural history of the Midwestern regional landscape. The drainage swale functions as a "rain gauge," filling and absorbing runoff from frequent seasonal downpours. Osage orange hedgerows recall wind and snow control strategies beginning in the late 19th century. Cutting through working fields, the tree-lined parkway refers to county road improvements of the 1930s, and so on.

Recalling how quickly the design was produced, Terry trenchantly remarks: "I did this in a week for the Chancellor who wanted a design ... they already had the architect and so I turned it around that quickly. But it was so threatening to the campus planner that he wouldn't even think about it." It might have been so glorious.

Stories like these only make Terry's dedication to tending his campus gardens and the increase in his recent activities on campus all the more meaningful. At the Gelvin Garden for example, his cheerfully determined efforts to introduce more native perennials into hybrid garden compositions have resulted in a subtle blend of prairie forbs and grasses with colorful exotics and annuals. Native sedums, yarrow, coneflower, rudbeckia, little bluestem grasses, and Joe Pye weed coexist happily beside fulsome exotics. With a tiny glint of sly glee, Terry confesses to a bit of guerrilla gardening, having slipped in a few plugs of native Prairie Dock in startling silhouette against the white marble façade of the Museum. To his dismay, a volunteer gardener diligently weeded it all out. But is there really any doubt he will try it again?

Left: Terry Harkness, n.d. Mixing natives with exotic perennials in the Gelvin Gardens (photo courtesy of Julia Kelly, July 2015)

Afterword

Robert B. Riley

For years I taught a course on the ordinary (read common, non-designed, or vernacular) landscape of America, mostly to students from architecture or landscape architecture. Often students would tell me that they enjoyed the course and understood the issues, but were not sure what it had to do with landscape architecture or with design. My answer was that sometimes it does. "Look at Terry Harkness's work," I said.

Terry's body of work now extends over fifty years. It defies characterization. It is broad and diverse, not specialized. It follows no trends, no fashions, no style nor group, no hero figures. But it does have some distinctive elements. Certainly he uses old materials and traditional forms in a new way. For the Midwest agrarian landscape his vocabulary includes *allées* leading from road to farmhouse, orientation obedient to the omnipresent surrounding grid, indigenous plants and trees, a fascination with the form of the swales in the wet season, and such details as hog wire fencing.

Terry is probably best understood as a regionalist designer. Regional design is one of those concepts always hanging about on the fringes of architectural and landscape architecture, never quite becoming fashionable nor a dominant concern. It is not easy to precisely identify what makes Terry's work different from the mundane historical kitsch usually advanced as regional. After over three decades of knowing and working with him I still can't quite express that particular essence that sets it apart. His work is not literal. Neither is it an abstraction clothed in *au courant* cant.

Terry's intense inquiry into region and history dates back as far as his MLA thesis at the University of Illinois in the late 1960s—a history of the east central Illinois landscape running from the retreat of

Above: *Prairie Native Culture—Curve (photo courtesy of Ken McCown, June 2008)*

Opposite: *Up square (photo courtesy of Ken McCown, March 2012)*

the glaciers to the coming of the railroads. The thesis format combines text and graphics in roughly equal proportions, each occupying half of a two-column page (a 'radical' format that required special university approval at the time). The text is solid, plain, and free of academic jargon. But ah! the drawings! Revelatory ink sketches capture every essential, every nuance of landscape change, in a distinctive drawing style that has served him well for decades.

That thread in Terry's work reached its climax almost a quarter of a century later in "An East Central Illinois Garden: A Regional Garden," a project included in Michael Van Valkenburgh's exhibition and catalog *Transforming the American Garden: 12 New Landscape Designs* (1986). Terry's "garden" is a contemporary farmstead. The buildings cluster together on a slight rise near the center of the land just as they do on the earliest farms in East Central Illinois. The house connects to the road by an allée of trees. It is early Spring, the trees are bare, the fields are mostly empty and sometimes flooded. But the essence of the design lies in two details.

Below and opposite: Terry Harkness, n.d. Details of swimming pool from An East Central Illinois Garden

In the northwest corner of the farmstead are two right triangles of standing water separated by a retaining wall. The center walls are arrow-straight and perpendicular while the hypotenuse is defined by a gentle sensuous curve of water, defining the shape of the swale with an immediacy no topographic map could match. The other tiny but defining detail is the swimming pool (this is after all the 1980s, not the 1850s). How many others could design a circular pool of gloss-enameled blue, emerging from the ground like a decapitated Harvestore silo, and not have it come on as kitsch? The proof is in the seeing.

Terry is also a blatant and unashamed plantsman, another theme persistent in landscape design but never quite fashionable or mainstream. Terry is the product of an American education system that graduates students knowing maybe one third of the number of plant species that their European counterparts learn. His love and knowledge of plants comes from decades of impassioned involvement, and close observation, rather than from curriculum. Terry cares about how plants grow and change. So do we all, I hope, but not very many of us have the drive and energy to build our professional life around that concern. It is his and his alone.

When Terry designs he is in it for the long run. Admirable, to be sure: how many of us can come up with the intent and the energy to keep walking a single site for years? He will not even have photographs of his work taken in the first years of a sites' development, an indicator of a rare designer. To Terry, maintenance is just as important as that first conceptual sketch, an integral part of landscape design. I have sometimes looked out my window and wondered who that person with yellow construction helmet was, wandering around my yard, far from any utilities. Of course it would be Terry, checking up as always to see what was happening with the ash trees, pruning here and there, sometimes removing a plant or suggesting an addition, always with a clean and clear concept dictating his interventions.

One way to sum up is to share part of what I wrote over a decade ago for Terry's nomination for the Jot Carpenter teaching medal: "Put simply, Terry has been the heart and soul of [the Illinois] program for close to four decades ... Even when he was on his several-year sabbatical to enter practice, we expected, hoped for his return. He is the bridge between students, even faculty, and the world of practice and teaching." (20 June, 2017)

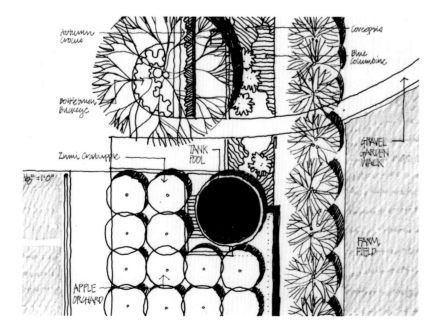

Contributors

Molly Catherine Briggs is Instructor in Art & Design as well as a doctoral candidate in landscape architecture history and theory at the University of Illinois at Urbana-Champaign. She holds an MFA in studio art from Northwestern University and has been the recipient of numerous creative and research awards, including the Douglas Dockery Thomas Fellowship in Garden History and Design and a Summer Fellowship at Dumbarton Oaks Research Library. She has also been recognized for outstanding contributions to teaching. Her dissertation, *Immersive Media and the Large Parks Movement*, identifies representational affinities between panoramas—painted virtual reality environments—and the large urban landscape parks that emerged simultaneously in the nineteenth century.

Brenda J. Brown teaches in the University of Manitoba's Department of Landscape Architecture. Her MLA degree (University of Illinois at Urbana Champaign, 1996) followed MA and MFA degrees from the University of Iowa. Together with Terry Harkness and Doug Johnston, she organized the Eco-Revelatory Design exhibition that opened at the University of Illinois at Urbana-Champaign in 1998 and closed at the National Building Museum in Washington, DC in 2000 and was editor of its catalogue. As designer, artist, writer, and educator, she continues to be concerned with the revelation of landscape ecosystem phenomena, processes, and relationships—particularly with reciprocal revelations of landscapes and sounds—in projects ranging from Florida to Manitoba to Michoacán.

Frank C. Clements, FASLA, received his MLA from the University of Illinois at Champaign-Urbana (1971) and his BS in Landscape Architecture from Michigan State University (1965). His working experience in landscape architecture, planning, and urban design spans 45 years at notable Midwestern firms such as HOK Architects (St. Louis) where he worked with Terry Harkness. He also worked at Johnson, Johnson and & Roy, Hitchcock Design Group, and Wolff Clements and Associates (Chicago). Clements has been involved in a wide variety of national and international projects, including national and community parks, office parks, office buildings, corporate headquarters and campuses, industrial facilities, housing complexes, urban and suburban streetscapes, and large mixed-use developments.

M. Elen Deming, ASLA, is Professor of Landscape Architecture at the University of Illinois, Urbana-Champaign, where she teaches design studio, history and theory, and research design. From 1993 to 2008, she taught at the State University of New York (SUNY) College of Environmental Science and Forestry, where she also co-edited *Landscape Journal*. A licensed landscape architect and cultural historian, Elen recently edited the book *Values in Landscape Architecture: Finding Center in Theory and Practice* (LSU 2015) and has published essays in several scholarly journals. Her co-authored book, *Landscape Architecture Research: Inquiry/ Strategy/ Design* (Wiley 2011), describes the breadth of research strategies advancing the field of practice.

***Opposite:** University of Illinois at Urbana-Champaign (photo courtesy of Ken McCown, June 2016)*

Kathleen Harleman, Acting Dean of the College of Fine & Applied Arts at the University of Illinois, Urbana-Champaign, has also served as Director of Krannert Art Museum (KAM) since 2004. She obtained her BA (Art History) from Middlebury College, MA (Art History) from Johns Hopkins University, and MBA from the University of Ottawa. Her thirty years of museum experience include appointments at several prestigious public and academic art institutions. These include work at the National Gallery of Canada and the Art Gallery of Ontario, leadership roles at Wellesley College's art museum and public museums in the Fort Lauderdale, FL and Seattle, WA areas, and consultancy with the Canadian Centre for Architecture in Montreal. For more than a decade, Kathleen has worked closely with Terry Harkness and others to curate and steward the KAM garden.

Founding principal and partner at Reed-Hilderbrand, **Gary Hilderbrand** FASLA is a renowned practitioner, teacher, critic, and writer, as well as Professor in Practice at the Harvard Graduate School of Design where he received his MLA degree and has taught since 1990. He received his BLA from the SUNY College of Environmental Science & Forestry, in Syracuse. Hilderbrand's honors include Harvard University's Charles Eliot Traveling Fellowship, The Rome Prize in Landscape Architecture, and ASLA's 2013 Firm of the Year Award. Co-author of *Visible/Invisible*, a monograph on his work, his published contributions include two other books and several essays. His deftly integrated career has helped position landscape architecture as a mediator between intellectual ideas and cultural traditions on the one hand, and contemporary forces of urbanization and change on the other.

Douglas M. Johnston, PhD, is Professor & Chair of Landscape Architecture at the SUNY College of Environmental Science & Forestry, where he received dual degrees in Environmental Studies and Landscape Architecture. After completing an MLA from Harvard, Johnston earned a PhD in Civil and Environmental Engineering from the University of Washington in Water Resources Planning and Management. He began teaching at the University of Illinois, Urbana-Champaign in 1986. Former Director of the Geographic Modeling Systems Laboratory at UIUC and Senior Research Scientist at the NCSA, he also chaired the Department of Landscape Architecture and Department of Community and Regional Planning at Iowa State University before returning to SUNY ESF. Johnston has been a prolific contributor to large-scale research on visualization software and its applications in landscape planning. Among his many publications, he co-authored the *Emiquon Preserve Visitor Use Plan* (2005-06) and *The Lake Michigan Shoreline Preserve Study* (2006) with Terry Harkness.

Since 2016, **Ken McCown**, ASLA, Associate AIA, IFLI, is Professor in the Fay Jones School of Architecture at the University of Arkansas where he serves as Department Head for Landscape Architecture and Adjunct Professor of Architecture. His background includes an undergraduate degree in landscape architecture and a graduate degree in architecture from the University of Illinois at Urbana-Champaign. These degrees provided a platform for integrative inquiry into the built environment through ecological literacy, transition/resilience design, ergonomic/behavior design, and urban design. After studying with Terry Harkness in the 1990s, McCown was a collaborator on the Foothills Mountain Observatory and served as faculty colleague and project designer on the Taj Mahal National Park and Cultural Heritage project.

Robert B. Riley is Professor *emeritus* and former Head (1970-1985) of the Department of Landscape Architecture at the University of Illinois, Urbana-Champaign. Beloved teacher, essayist, and thought leader, he is also a scholar of cultural and vernacular landscape studies. Riley's early work ran in *Landscape*, a journal founded by his mentor, the landscape geographer J. B. Jackson. Riley later edited *Landscape Journal* at the University of Illinois from 1988 to 1995 and co-edited the book *Theme Park Landscapes: Antecedents and Variations* (Dumbarton Oaks, 2002). Riley's collected essays *The Camaro in the Pasture* (UVA Press, 2015) won the John Brinckerhoff Jackson Prize in 2016.

Amita Sinha, PhD is Professor of Landscape Architecture at the University of Illinois at Urbana-Champaign. She links her expertise in ethnography of public space with her studio design pedagogy. Her major scholarly focus is on the cultural landscapes of South Asia, the subject of *Landscapes In India: Forms and Meanings* (Colorado University Press, 2006) reprinted by Asia Educational Services (2011). Sinha is also editor of *Landscape Perception* (Academic Press, 1995) and *Natural Heritage of Delhi* (USIEF and INTACH, 2009), and co-editor of *Cultural Landscapes of South Asia: Studies in Heritage Conservation and Management* (Routledge, 2017). Her articles have been published in numerous prestigious journals.

Below: Storm Coming (photo courtesy of Ken McCown, March 2012)

James Wescoat is Aga Khan Professor of Islamic Architecture at the School of Architecture, MIT, and former Head of the Landscape Architecture Department at the University of Illinois, Urbana-Champaign (2002-2008). Wescoat's research focuses on water systems in the United States and South Asia from site scale to river basins, from Colorado to the Indus Valley. While at Illinois he worked closely with Amita Sinha, D. Fairchild Ruggles, and Gary Kesler on the Champaner-Pavagadh project in Gujarat, India. He is co-editor of *Political Economies of Landscape Changes: Places of Integrative Power* with Doug Johnston (Springer, 2007), and *Mughal Gardens: Sources, Places, Representations, Prospects* (Dumbarton Oaks, 1996). He co-authored *Water for Life: Water Management and Environmental Policy* with Gilbert F. White (Cambridge University, 2003).

CV & REPRESENTATIVE PROJECTS

Terence G. Harkness, FASLA

Registered Landscape Architect (Illinois)

Landscape Architecture | Land Planning | Garden Design

Champaign IL

Education

Coursework 1959-60. California State Polytechnic University at Pomona

Military Service 1960-62. United States Army, Monterey CA

BFA 1966. University of Illinois at Urbana-Champaign

MLA 1970. University of Illinois at Urbana-Champaign

Academic Practice

1969-1973. Assistant Professor of Landscape Architecture,
University of Illinois at Urbana-Champaign

1981-2007. Professor of Landscape Architecture,
University of Illinois at Urbana-Champaign

1998. Jens Jensen Visiting Professorship in Landscape Urbanism.
School of Architecture, University of Illinois at Chicago

2007-present. Professor *emeritus* of Landscape Architecture,
University of Illinois at Urbana-Champaign

Professional Practice

1960. Landscape Intern at M. Meade Palmer, FASLA. Warrenton, VA (summer)

1962-64. Landscape Designer at Courtland Paul | Arthur Beggs & Associates
Landscape Architecture & Planning, Corona del Mar, CA (also summers 1965-66;
1968-70).

1973-74. Landscape Architect at Peridean Group, Newport Beach, CA
*At Peridean, Harkness was responsible for design development, project scale site
development, and land planning for the Irvine Company, Newport Beach, CA.*

1974-1981. Senior Vice President of Planning and Landscape Architecture Division,
Hellmuth, Obata and Kassabaum (HOK), Inc. St. Louis, MO
*At HOK, Harkness served as director of design for a collaborative landscape
architecture studio of 35 persons including landscape architects, architects, planners,
and urban designers.*

1981-present. Landscape Architecture & Planning Consultant
*Harkness maintains an independent consulting practice working at all scales across
many regions of the country.*

Professional & Academic Awards

1968. Edward L. Ryerson Traveling Fellowship (Japan). Dept. of Landscape
Architecture, University of Illinois at Urbana-Champaign

1978. American Society of Landscape Architects (ASLA) Honor Award for
Laclede's Landing Urban Design Guidelines (HOK, Inc.)

1978. ASLA Merit Award for Lake Placid 1980 Winter Olympics Comprehensive Plan
(HOK, Inc.)

1978. *Urban Design* magazine Historic Preservation Award for
Laclede's Landing Redevelopment Plan (HOK, Inc.)

1980. American Planning Association (APA) Honor Award in Urban Design for
Laclede's Landing Redevelopment Plan (HOK, Inc.)

1987. ASLA (Illinois Chapter) Merit Award for design folio *Historic Precedent/Design
Research/Landscape Design* [Illinois garden series]

1990. Council of Educators in Landscape Architecture (CELA)
Outstanding Educator Award

1994. Elevation to Fellow of the ASLA

1994. ASLA (Illinois Chapter) Honor Award for "The Workingman's Garden" with
Doug Johnston

1994. Arnold O. Beckman Award for traveling exhibition and catalog "Eco-revelatory
Design: Nature Constructed/Nature Revealed" with Brenda Brown and Doug
Johnston. Campus Research Board, University of Illinois at
Urbana-Champaign

1995. Graham Foundation Grant awarded for exhibition and catalog "Eco-revelatory
Design: Nature Constructed/Nature Revealed" with Brenda Brown and Doug
Johnston

1999. ASLA Merit Award for traveling exhibition and *Landscape Journal* catalog "Eco-
revelatory Design: Nature Constructed/Nature Revealed" with Brenda Brown and
Doug Johnston

2002. ASLA Merit Award for Taj Mahal Cultural Heritage District Development Plan,
Dept. of Landscape Architecture, University of Illinois at Urbana-Champaign
(with V. Bellafiore, K. McCown, B. Orland, and A. Sinha) and Directorate of Tourism,
Uttar Pradesh, India

2005. Selected to serve on the ASLA National Awards Jury, Washington, DC

2007. Jot Carpenter Teaching Medal, *awarded annually by the ASLA for sustained and
significant contributions to excellence in landscape architecture education*

Representative Projects

Landscape Design & Preservation (with HOK, Inc. St. Louis)

1975. *Site design*. University Library at Western Illinois University, Macomb, IL

1977. *Prairie establishment*. John Deere Equipment Engineering Facility, Davenport, IA

1978. *Prairie thicket border*. Cities Service Technological Center, Tulsa, OK

1978. *Woodland restoration*. Ashland Coal Headquarters, Huntington, WV

1979. *Historic building and campus preservation*. School of Management at
Vanderbilt University, Nashville, TN (with HOK Inc. Nashville office)

1979. *Preservation and development of monastery and landscape*.
GTE Corporate Executive Training Center, Norwalk, CN

1980. *Farmland preservation*. Exxon Research and Engineering Facility, Clinton NJ

1980-83. *Commons courtyard garden and fountain*.
McDonnell Douglas Information Services Co.

1981. *Preservation of Victorian walking park and senior citizen center.* Stupp Memorial Garden, Community Center in Tower Grove Park, City of St. Louis, MO

1981-83. *Library plaza and fountain; Parrington Oval and new campus.* University of Oklahoma Campus Master Plan, Norman. OK

Landscape Design & Preservation (consulting and UIUC studio projects)

1981-83. *Landscape reclamation of two sewage treatment lagoons and 2 landfills into a 100-acre park with a 20-acre lake.* Chanute Air Force Base, Rantoul, IL

1989-90. *Outdoor sculpture and perennial garden.* The Gelvin Garden, Krannert Art Museum at the University of Illinois at Urbana-Champaign

1992-93. *Schematic plan and plant collections alternatives.* University Arboretum (with students of the Dept. of Landscape Architecture, University of Illinois at Urbana-Champaign)

1992-93. Teaching and community arboretum. Myer Arboretum at Southern Illinois University, Edwardsville IL (with students of the Dept. of Landscape Architecture, University of Illinois at Urbana-Champaign)

1993. *Restoration planting options for Armour estate (Mellody Farm).* Formal Gardens at Lake Forest Academy, Lake Forest IL (with students of the Dept. of Landscape Architecture, University of Illinois at Urbana-Champaign)

1993-2003. *Woodland, grassland, and farmland restoration of rural landscape for 84-acre site.* Phases I to IV, Great Plains Software Research, Development, and Production Facility, Fargo, ND (joint venture with M. Torgerson, with McClier Architecture & Engineering, and Julie Snow Architects)

1995-2009. *Campus development, site design, garden groves, and arboretum elements on 55-acre site.* Microsoft Fargo Corporate Research and Service Center, Fargo, ND (with Julie Snow Architects, and Perkins & Will Architects)

1996. *Woodland ravine restoration.* Environmental Education and Visitor Center at Scovill Park & Decatur Zoo. Decatur Park District, Decatur IL

1997. *Planting plan and courtyard fountain design.* New Science Center & Watson Laboratory Complex, Principia College, Elsah IL (with S. Dawson, Sasaki Associates, Watertown, MA)

2003. *Woodland preservation and management plan.* Microsoft/Great Plains/Solomon Group Software Development Facility, Findlay OH

2005. *Visitor use plan.* Emiquon Preserve, Havana IL. The Nature Conservancy - Illinois State Office (with Austin Tao Associates and D. Johnston)

2006. *Ravine, bluff, and shoreline restoration and nature preserve.* Openlands Lakeshore Preserve, Highwood/Fort Sheridan IL. Chicago Openlands (with D. Johnston)

2012. *Planting plan and site design.* School of Nations, School of Government, and Core Academic Building. Principia College, Elsah, IL (with Powers Bowersox architects and John Guenther)

Urban Design, Development & Historic Preservation (with HOK, Inc. St. Louis, MO)

1975-1981. *Master development plan, design guidelines, streetscape design, and graphic development.* Laclede's Landing Redevelopment Corporation, St. Louis, MO

1981. *Redevelopment of historic 1903 train station.* Union Station Feasibility Study, Rouse Company and Omni Hotels, St. Louis, MO

Urban Design, Development & Historic Preservation (consulting projects)

1984. *Urban design guidelines.* Wharfside Redevelopment Corporation & Land Clearance Authority, City of St. Louis MO (with Powers Associates, Inc.)

1985-2000. *Urban design & community redevelopment planning consultant.* City of St. Louis, Lacledes Landing Foundation, and Wharfside Redevelopment Corporation, St. Louis MO

2000. *Public arts framework and strategies for the St. Louis waterfront.* The Whitaker Foundation and Lacledes Redevelopment Corporation (with B. Chen)

2004. *Courthouse Square and downtown design guidelines.* Kirksville, MO (with Powers Bowersox Architects)

2009-10. *Community Land Use Strategies.* Carondelet Community Betterment Federation and Carondelet Housing Corporation, St Louis, MO (with T. Purcell, neighborhood redevelopment consulting specialist)

Community Master Planning & Open Space Planning (consulting and studio projects)

1974. *Baldwin Hills Park Master Plan.* LA County Parks and Recreation, Los Angeles CA (with Peridean Group)

1974. *Site selection and master planning for 287-acre site.* Aetna Life and Casualty Group Headquarters. Middletown, CN

1974-75. *Alaska State Capitol site selection study.* Willow, AK (with HOK, Inc. San Francisco, CA / Anchorage, AK)

1978. *Convention and community center design.* Decatur Civic Center, Decatur IL (with HOK, Inc. and BSLD Associates)

1982-84. *Basewide play facilities assessment and development program (1982); Outdoor recreation plan (1983); wildlife and conservation plan (1984).* Chanute Air Force Base, Rantoul IL (with Illinois State Dept. of Conservation and Dept. of Recreation and Leisure Studies, University of Illinois at Urbana-Champaign)

1983. *"Phoenix Park: Design, Behavior and Environment," new neighborhood park design.* Longview Housing Project, Decatur Park District, Decatur Public Housing Authority (with the Housing Research & Development research program at the University of Illinois at Urbana-Champaign, and Bradley, Salogga, Likens, and Dillow Architects, AIA)

1987-88. *Comprehensive base plan.* Air Force Headquarters Command, Randolph Air Force Base, San Antonio TX (with MSE Inc., Indianapolis)

1988. *Development plan and architectural prototypes for residential treatment center.* Voelkerding Village in Dutzow, MO, a Lutheran Association, Dakota Boys Ranch Foundation, Minot ND

1988. *Preservation & development plan for an original site of Buddha: Buddha's First Sermon.* Ministry of Tourism, Sarnath, Uttar Pradesh, India (with the US Embassy, National Park Service, and Dept. of Landscape Architecture, University of Illinois at Urbana-Champaign)

1989. *Residential and new golf community recreation plan for Lynwood Farms.* Browning Investment, Carmel IN (with MSE, Indianapolis)

1989-90. *Neighborhood conservation and neighborhood park program.* Conoco Community Interface Plan, Conoco Petroleum, Ponco City, OK (with Cannon Associates, St. Louis)

1990. *Planning issues and development strategies report*. Convention Center Expansion New Stadium Project, St. Louis MO (with Development Strategies, Inc | LLRC Corp. | Wharfside Redevelopment Corporation)

1991. *Neighborhood protection and refinery land management strategies*. Mobil/ Torrance Community Interface Plan, Mobil Refinery, Torrance CA (with Cannon Associates, St. Louis)

1992-99. *Preservation and acquisition of community floodway, forestlands, and parkland with development of adjacent parkway system*. Forsyth Floodway, Greenway, and Open Space Plan, Village of Forsyth, IL

2002–2004. *Glacial and land use history of Lake Agassiz Region*. Burgum Riverbend Farms Interpretive Center. Red River Valley of the North, States of Minnesota, North Dakota, and South Dakota (with M. Torgerson, Fargo)

2003. *Community treatment facility and school grounds*. Dakota Boys and Girls Ranch, Bismark, ND (with D. Schultz and A. Torgerson, AIA)

2003. *Preservation and re-use of portion of historic Minnesota State Mental Hospital including restoration of grounds and site plantings*. Ottertail County Civic Center, Fergus Falls, MN (with D. Schultz and A. Torgerson, AIA)

Landscape Design and Garden Theory in Practice (selected projects)

1968. *Pool/hedge and orchard garden*. Erickson Garden, South Pasadena, CA

1968. *Foothill terrace garden*. Fry Garden, Altadena, CA

1973. *Perennial border and native woodland ravine*. Funk Garden at Lake Decatur, Decatur IL

1979. *Oak woodland and shade garden*. Johnston Garden, Glendale MO

1981-1986. *Development of parkland taking rural Illinois landscape as a model. Restoration of Illinois landscapes and recreational use of waste disposal and sewage lagoon sites*. Chanute Air Force Base, Rantoul, IL

1994. *The Workingman's Garden*. D. Johnston Garden, Champaign, IL

1995. *Courtyard gardens*. J. and J. Liebman Gardens, Urbana, IL

N.B. Project details are compiled from several archival records and should be verified

SELECTED PUBLICATIONS

Published Works & Citations

Brown, B., with T. Harkness and D. Johnston, guest eds. 1998. *In Exhibition catalog for Eco-Revelatory Design: Nature Constructed/Nature Revealed*. Special Issue of Landscape Journal.
  • Brown, Harkness, and Johnston. "Proposal" (drafted ca. 1994), pp. x-xi.
  • ____. Guest Editors' Introduction," pp. xii-xv.
  • Haag, R. "Eco-Revelatory Design: The Challenge of the Exhibit," pp. 72-79.
  • Harkness, T. "Foothill Mountain Observatory: Golden Mountain Reconsidered," pp. 42-45.
  • Thayer, R. L., Jr. "Landscape as an Ecologically Revealing Language," pp. 118-129.

Harkness, T. 1970. *A Landscape in Evolution: The Graphic History of Champaign and Piatt Counties from 70,000 BC to AD 1860*. MLA Thesis. Department of Landscape Architecture, University of Illinois, Urbana-Champaign.

____. 1986. "An East Central Illinois Garden: A Regional Garden." *Places: Transforming the American Garden*. Vol. 3, issue 3 (Winter), pp 6-9. https://placesjournal.org/print-archive/transforming-the-american-garden/ [permalink: http://escholarship.org/uc/item/5fn150b5]

____. 1988. "An East Central Illinois Garden: A Regional Garden," in Michael Van Valkenburgh, ed. *Transforming the American Garden: 12 New Landscape Designs*. Catalog. Cambridge, MA: Harvard University Graduate School of Design, pp. 40-43.

____. 1990. "Garden from Region." In The Meaning of Gardens: Idea, Place and Action, ed. Mark Francis and Randolph T. Hester, Jr. Cambridge, MA: MIT Press, pp. 110-119.

____. 1990. "Landscape Stories," pp 42 in *Landscapes for the 21st Century* [juried ideas competition], *Landscape Architecture Magazine* vol 80, no 12 (December), pp 32-56.

____. 1993. "Most Influential Landscapes." *Landscape Journal* vol. 12 (Fall), pp 176-177.

____. 2002. "Garden from Region" reprint in chapter *Integrating Site, Place, and Region*. In *Theory in Landscape Architecture: a Reader*, ed. Simon Swaffield. Philadelphia: University of Pennsylvania Press, pp. 216-219.

____. 2003. "Pilgrimmage to Agra: A Cultural Heritage Landscape," pp. 76-79 in theme issue "Research: The Taj Mahal Precincts." *Architecture + Design: A Journal of Indian Architecture* 20:6 (Nov-Dec), guest ed. A. Sinha (compilation/publication of research by invitation of the Uttar Pradesh tourism department).

____. 2004. "Distilling North Dakota: Can Landscape Architecture Reflect the Essence of Regional Landscapes?" *Landscape Architecture Magazine* vol 84, no 4 (April), p. 66

Harkness, T and D. Johnston. 1994. "The Workingman's Garden." Unpublished ms submitted for ASLA (Illinois Chapter) Honor Award in Landscape Design.

Krog, S. 1991. "Whither the Garden?" In *Denatured Visions: Landscape and Culture in the Twentieth Century*. New York: Museum of Modern Art (Terry Harkness work cited pp. 103-4)

Moorhead, Steven, ed. 1997. *Landscape Architecture*. Gloucester, Mass.: Rockport. (Terry Harkness work cited pp. 88-93)

Sinha, A. and T. Harkness. 2009. "Views of the Taj: Figure in the Landscape." *Landscape Journal*, pp. 198-217

Tao (Austin) & Associates, Office of Terry Harkness, and Doug Johnston. January 2006. *Emiquon Preserve Visitor Use Plan: Executive Summary*. The Nature Conservancy

Treib, M. 1986. "On Paper and Plants [An Exhibition Debate]." In *Places Journal— Transforming the American Garden: 12 New Landscape Designs*. Exhibition entries & respondents, pp. 56-59 [permalink: http://escholarship.org/uc/item/30z662n4]

Unpublished Design Research: Exhibitions, Lectures, Presentations, and White Papers

Harkness, T. 1985. "Searching for a Middle West Garden: Historic Precedent in Design." Conference paper presented at Annual Meeting of the Council of Educators in Landscape Architecture (CELA), University of Illinois at Urbana-Champaign, IL (Fall)

____. 1986. "The Cultural Landscape and Design: The Use and Meaning of the Vernacular Rural Landscape for Landscape Architecture." Conference paper presented at Annual Meeting of CELA, University of Virginia at Charlottesville, VA (Spring)

____. 1986. "An East Central Illinois Garden: The Regional Landscape as the Source for an Approach to Landscape Design." Colloquium lecture presented at the Graduate School of Design, Harvard University, Cambridge MA (Spring)

____. 1986. "An East Central Illinois Garden: A Regional Garden." Exhibit for *Transforming the American Garden: New Directions in Landscape Architecture*, symposium and traveling exhibition (1986—88) organized by Michael Van Valkenburgh, Graduate School of Design, Harvard University, Cambridge MA

____. 1987. "The Common Landscape: A Garden and Meaning." Conference paper presented for *Meanings of the Garden*, Center for Design Research, University of California at Davis (May)

____. 1987. "Landscape Design and the Common Landscape: Presence and Response." Plenary speaker for *Charting New Paths*—Annual Meeting of CELA, Rhode Island School of Design, Providence RI (August)

____. 1987. "Garden Design and the Common Landscape: Continuity and Change." Invited speaker for International Federation of Landscape Architects (IFLA) World Congress, Paris (September)

____. 1987. "*Un Jardin en Illinois: Jardins, Continuité et Création*." Translation by Isabelle Auricoste at the symposium *Paysage et Amenagement*, Limoges France (December)

____. 1988. *Design Research: Landscape Design and the Common Landscape*. unpublished ms. Department of Landscape Architecture, University of Illinois, Urbana-Champaign
  • Background Research: A Regional Landscape
  • Design Application I: A Midwest Garden
  • Design Application II: An Urban Garden
  • Design Application III: A Midwestern Regional Airport

____. 1988. "Reading the American Landscape: Design and the Common Landscape." Conference paper for *The Regional Landscape*, symposium held at Rutgers University, New Brunswick, NJ (September)

____. 1988. "Landscape Design and the Regional Context: Landscape into Design— Three Regional Studies." Bracken Lecturer at Penn State University, State College, PA (November)

____. 1989. "The Illinois Landscape and Landscape Design." Invited lecture for the Chicago Architectural Club, Graham Foundation, Chicago IL (April)

____. 1990. "The Prairie Swale as Design Metaphor: Design for the South Garden of the Krannert Art Museum." Unpublished design proposal presented to University administrators, University of Illinois at Urbana-Champaign

____. 1990. "Landscape Design: The Common Landscape, Presence and Response, Continuity and Change." Unpublished ms. Department of Landscape Architecture, University of Illinois, Urbana-Champaign

____. 1990. "Landscape Stories II: Airport/ Gateway/ Portal—Landscape as Interpretive History." Unpublished design proposal for Willard Airport presented to University administrators, University of Illinois at Urbana-Champaign (Summer)

____. 1991. "Infinite Space: Bounded/Unbounded Space and Garden Paradoxes— The Midwest Garden Series." Department of Landscape Architecture, University of Illinois, Urbana-Champaign

____. 1992. "The New American Garden." Invited lecture for the Spring Garden Lecture Series, Minnesota Landscape Arboretum, Chanahausen, MN (Spring)

____. 1993. "Farmland/Shelterbelt as Landscape Design Precedent." Unpublished landscape design proposal presented to Great Plains Software Research and Development Facility, Fargo ND

____. 1995. "Sabbatical Leave of Absence Proposal." unpublished white paper. Department of Landscape Architecture, University of Illinois, Urbana-Champaign

____. 1995-96. "Foothill Gardens: New Lives—New Landscapes, a Series." *Lecture/ exhibitions on interpretive hydrology program for visitors' center; proposal for Flood Control/Engineering section of LA County Public Works*. Presented at University of Toronto, University of Guelph and the University of Montréal, Canada (Fall)

____. 1998. "Landscape Observatories." Jens Jenson Visiting Lecture, School of Architecture, University of Illinois at Chicago

____. 1998-2000. Gallery talks given for "Eco-Revelatory Design: Nature Constructed/ Nature Revealed" traveling exhibition shown at
  • University of Illinois Urbana-Champaign (Fall 1998)
  • Chicago Botanic Garden (Spring 1999)
  • ASLA/Boston Architectural Center (Fall 1999)
  • Iowa State University Symposium (Spring 2000)
  • National Building Museum, Smithsonian Institution (Summer 2000)

____. 2003. "Design Strategies for Landscape Interpretation." Conference paper presented for *Cultural Landscapes of the Inland Empire*, symposium held by Department of Architecture, California State Polytechnic University at Pomona (Spring)

____. 2011. "Four Interviews: Conversations between Terry Harkness, Molly C. Briggs, and M. Elen Deming." Unpublished transcripts, Department of Landscape Architecture, University of Illinois at Urbana-Champaign

N.B. Numerous other undated, unpublished essays, drawings, correspondence, project reports, syllabi, teaching problems, slides, and student projects are held in the personal archive of Terence G. Harkness.

Book Design
Elizabeth Vogel

Photography
Brenda J. Brown
Terry G. Harkness
Misa Inoue
Julia Kelly
Ken McCown
James Steinkamp
Elizabeth Vogel